VOCABULARY
for Achievement

Grade 5

D1558343

Margaret Ann Richek

GREAT SOURCE
WILMINGTON, MA

Margaret Ann Richek

Professor, College of Education, Northeastern Illinois University; consultant in reading and vocabulary study; author of *The World of Words* (Houghton Mifflin)

Writing and Editing: Maryann Langen, Cara Lieb, Sue Paro

Text Design and Production: Publicom, Inc.

Illustrations: Rita Lascaro and Carol Maglitta

Cover Design: Publicom, Inc.

Cover Photo: Stone/Stuart Westmorland

Acknowledgments

The pronunciation key and the dictionary entries on pages 21-24 and 58-59: Copyright © 1998 by Houghton Mifflin Company. Reproduced by permission from THE AMERICAN HERITAGE CHILDREN'S DICTIONARY.

Thesaurus entries on pages 81 and 84: Copyright © 1997 by Paul Hellweg. Reproduced by permission from THE AMERICAN HERITAGE CHILDREN'S THESAURUS.

Printed in the United States

International Standard Book Number: 0-669-47131-3

1 2 3 4 5 6 7 8 9 10 - POO - 05 04 03 02 01 00

Teacher's Edition Contents

About *Vocabulary for Achievement* iv
Complete Grade 5 Word List xv
Vocabulary Skills in *Vocabulary for Achievement* xvi

PLAYING WITH WORDS

Lesson 1   **SKILL LESSON:** synonyms, parts of speech 1
Lesson 2   To All Appearances: words about how things look 5
Lesson 3   In Character: words about people 9
Lesson 4   Picture This: words that tell about setting 13
Lesson 5   **REVIEW:** Lessons 1–4 17

WORKING WITH WORDS

Lesson 6   **SKILL LESSON:** using the dictionary 21
Lesson 7   Just the Right Word: parts of speech 25
Lesson 8   Double Duty: words that are both nouns and verbs 29
Lesson 9   Same but Different: words with multiple meanings 33
Lesson 10   **REVIEW:** Lessons 6–9 37

THINKING WITH WORDS

Lesson 11   **SKILL LESSON:** using context 41
Lesson 12   Words for a New Nation: words from social studies 45
Lesson 13   Making Sense: words from science 49
Lesson 14   Traditional Tales: words from myths 53
Lesson 15   **REVIEW:** Lessons 11–14 57

FORMING NEW WORDS

Lesson 16   **SKILL LESSON:** prefixes and suffixes 61
Lesson 17   Under and Over: prefixes *sub-* and *super-* 65
Lesson 18   "Not" Again!: prefixes *in-, il-, im-* 69
Lesson 19   One, Two, Three . . . : prefixes *uni-, bi-, tri-* 73
Lesson 20   **REVIEW:** Lessons 16–19 77

GOING BEYOND WORDS

Lesson 21   **SKILL LESSON:** using a thesaurus 81
Lesson 22   Good or Bad?: shades of meaning 85
Lesson 23   It's All Greek: words from ancient Greek 89
Lesson 24   Great Advice: proverbs 93
Lesson 25   **REVIEW:** Lessons 21–24 97

LOOKING INTO WORDS

Lesson 26   **SKILL LESSON:** prefixes, suffixes, and roots 101
Lesson 27   Opposite "Dis-": prefix *dis-* 105
Lesson 28   Across the Way: prefix *trans-* 109
Lesson 29   Around and Around: word parts *ambi-, amphi, circu-* 113
Lesson 30   **REVIEW:** Lessons 26–29 117

Test: Lessons 1–5 125
Test: Lessons 6–10 127
Test: Lessons 11–15 129
Test: Lessons 16–20 131
Test: Lessons 21–25 133
Test: Lessons 26–30 135

About Vocabulary for Achievement

Why Teach Vocabulary?

It is a given that vocabulary instruction is an integral part of teaching students to read. But why is it necessary to teach vocabulary in the upper grades? After grade 3, students switch from learning to read to reading to learn. Because students need to read to acquire knowledge, vocabulary skills continue to be important to their success. The ability of students to comprehend what they read directly affects their performance in all subject areas. Good vocabulary skills can help students comprehend what they read, increase their ability to connect with and activate their own prior knowledge, and improve their ability to make correct inferences about unknown words. Research shows that the size of a student's vocabulary is a good predictor of comprehension. Therefore, the more words students can master, the better prepared they will be to

- understand what they read,

- write and speak well, and

- perform successfully on standardized tests.

Systematic vocabulary instruction provides the necessary framework for creating a multi-layered, language-rich environment. To effectively build vocabulary, students must be active participants in their learning. They must be able not only to find words in the dictionary, but also to define, in their own words, what a word means to them. Students need to engage in a variety of speaking, viewing, writing, listening, and even kinesthetic activities, in order to learn to appreciate, analyze, and internalize new words. The instruction in *Vocabulary for Achievement* involves students directly in these processes to help them recognize, develop, and use strategies for determining meanings and for using new words correctly.

How the Words Were Chosen

In choosing words for *Vocabulary for Achievement*, grades 3–5, we strove to select a core list of words that students would be able to use in reading and writing. We also wanted to select words that students could use as tools for expanding vocabulary and for developing higher-level thinking skills. The resulting list contains words that are

- appropriate in frequency of use, a measure that is highly correlated with the level of difficulty,

- useful in the subject areas (literature, social studies, science) for these grades,

- organized around important central concepts that students can connect with and expand upon as they acquire more words,

- easy to use as tools to acquire more sophisticated vocabulary concepts, such as using context, using reference sources (dictionary and thesaurus), using word parts (prefixes, suffixes, roots), and using parts of speech, and

- facilitative of higher-level thinking skills, such as solving analogies and making inferences about multiple meanings, idioms, and proverbs.

To compile information about word frequency, we consulted print and electronic databases. The most extensive and recent list of English usage is *Educator's Word Frequency Guide*, by Zeno et al. This list contains over seventeen million words, three times that of any previous list. We also consulted raw frequency, logarithmic transformations, and grade-level analyses. The frequencies we found were confirmed by comparing them with earlier databases, such as

Carroll, J.B., P. Davies, and B. Richman. *The American Heritage Word Frequency Book*. Boston: Houghton Mifflin Co., 1971.

Dale E., and J. O'Rourke. *The Living Word Vocabulary*. Chicago: World Book/Childcraft, 1981.

Harris, A. and M.D. Jacobson, *Basic Reading Vocabularies*. New York: Macmillan, 1982.

Kuçera, H., and W.N. Francis. *Computational Analysis of Present-Day American English*. Providence, RI: Brown University Press, 1967.

Thorndike, E.L., and I. Lorge. *The Teacher's Word Book of 30,000 Words*. New York: Teachers College Press, Columbia University, 1944.

Zeno, S.M., S.H. Ivens, R.T. Millard, and R. Durvuri, *The Educator's Word Frequency Guide*. Brewster, New York: Touchtone Applied Science Associates (TASA), 1995.

Practical Considerations for the Word Lists

The word lists for *Vocabulary for Achievement* were selected and organized with the following considerations in mind:

Appropriate Levels of Difficulty The statistics confirm that, as measured in frequency of use, the words chosen for *Vocabulary for Achievement* are of appropriate difficulty for each grade level.

Usefulness To help us choose words used in textbooks, novels, and other curricular material, we consulted databases in popular sources, such as newspapers, to estimate the usefulness of each word.

Central Concepts Because children often learn words by associating them with a central concept, the words introduced in *Vocabulary for Achievement* were chosen for their appropriateness in teaching concepts in curricular areas, as well as topics such as synonyms, prefixes, suffixes, and multiple meanings.

Student Input Classroom teaching experience is critical to developing a vocabulary program that will inspire them to learn words. The instruction in *Vocabulary for Achievement* is based on the author's classroom teaching experiences with third, fourth, and fifth grade students.

Teacher Input In addition, the thoughtful input of a diverse panel of teachers and administrators was critical to refining the final list.

The Structure of *Vocabulary for Achievement*

The 30 lessons in *Vocabulary for Achievement* are divided into 6 strands, or units, of 5 lessons each. Each unit opens with a lesson that focuses on particular skills or strategies. The central lessons of each unit introduce carefully chosen new words and provide opportunities for students to use the new words in a variety of activities. These 3 lessons are linked to the skills taught in the opening lesson. Each unit ends with a review lesson that gives students more practice with the new words and skills, as well as practice in test-taking skills.

Unit 1: Playing with Words

In the first unit, students will learn to appreciate how words relate to one another. The skill instruction focuses on word relationships and using alternative words. Students will develop flexibility in using and manipulating words as they learn about synonyms and parts of speech. The focus is on adjectives, as students learn words to describe appearances, characters, traits, and settings.

Unit 2: Working with Words

In this unit, students will work with four parts of speech—verbs, nouns, adjectives, and adverbs. Skill instruction focuses on understanding dictionary entries. In the lessons, students will explore words that can be used either as nouns or verbs. They will also apply strategies and dictionary skills to multiple-meaning words.

Unit 3: Thinking with Words

Many of the unfamiliar words students encounter will be in their content-area reading. This unit teaches words from social studies, science, and literature. The skill focus is on using context and dictionary as support tools for determining meanings of unfamiliar words.

Unit 4: Forming New Words

The ability to break a word into its parts (prefix, root, and suffix) is useful when attempting to decipher an unfamiliar word. The skill lesson introduces prefixes and suffixes used in the vocabulary words for this unit and discusses roots.

Unit 5: Going Beyond Words

Facility with language goes beyond the literal meanings of words. This unit introduces connotations and proverbs and delves into the origins of words from mythology. Support skills include using the thesaurus and the dictionary.

Unit 6: Looking into Words

Frequently words themselves hold the key to their meaning. Students must learn to look into a word to find parts that they recognize in order to figure out the meaning. This unit extends the work on prefixes and roots. Students learn how to find meaning within words.

Three Types of Lessons

The consistent structure of *Vocabulary for Achievement* makes it ideal for classroom instruction or for independent use, allowing you to direct a sound and successful vocabulary program. Teaching notes on the TE lesson pages give suggestions for introducing skills and strategies and for extending activities.

Skill Lessons

Each unit opens with a lesson that teaches important vocabulary skills and strategies. The skill lessons include abundant context, practice activities, and opportunities for application.

Word Lessons

Three lessons teach new words in each unit. A word lesson begins by introducing 8 words related by theme or concept, with pronunciations, parts of speech, definitions, and example sentences. A matching exercise reviews and reinforces the definitions of the new words. Next, a comprehension passage presents the words in context and follow-up questions check comprehension. Then exercises such as sentence completion, categorizing, and crossword puzzles provide meaningful practice in using the words. Finally, an Off the Page activity takes students beyond the book to explore words in a creative activity such as writing a paragraph or constructing a chart. To enhance instruction, two Enrichment Words may be introduced.

Review Lessons

Each unit ends with a review lesson that reviews the 24 new words plus the skill focus of the unit. Because they are optional, the Enrichment Words are reviewed in a separate activity. The review lessons also provide instruction and practice in test-taking skills for multiple-choice tests and analogies.

Testing

Six reproducible, standardized-format tests—one for each unit—are provided in the back of the Teacher's Edition. The tests are in multiple-choice format. Because the Enrichment Words are optional, they are tested in a separate section of each test.

Pacing

One lesson per week is the suggested pacing, but this may easily be adjusted to fit individual needs. Since vocabulary instruction is only a part of a complete language arts program, the lessons are designed to be brief and portable. Each lesson is printed on two pages, which can be torn out of the book and stapled together to use for the week.

Strategies for Teaching Vocabulary

The more active and involved your students are with words, the faster their vocabulary will grow. These strategies will help you support vocabulary instruction. The reproducible graphics on pages xii–xiv provide visual ways to put strategies into instant use.

Make Word Associations

One way to access students' prior knowledge and make explicit connections to new vocabulary is to **build a word web** for a vocabulary word. Place a key word in the center of the web (page xii) and record related words and concepts around the center. Constructing a web around a key vocabulary word provides an opportunity for students to make personal connections to the word as well as associations between words.

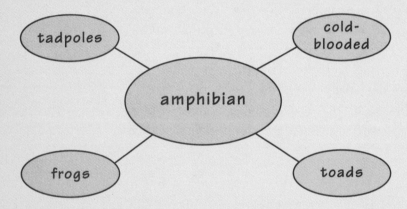

Explore Words

Another way of organizing thoughts and concepts about vocabulary words is to **make a T-chart.** (See page xiii.) The title of the chart is always the vocabulary word to be explored. To help students focus their thinking, you can supply the headings. Below is a T-chart for the word fragile, from Lesson 2. When students have finished their charts, have them share the results with the class and/or post the charts so that everyone can benefit from each child's thinking.

Fragile	
Things That Are Fragile	Other Words for Fragile
Crystal glasses	Delicate
Electronic equipment	Easily broken
Light bulbs	Thin

Develop Word Awareness

One of the best things a teacher can do for students is to develop their word awareness. Every time you come across a **"rich" word** in a book you are reading aloud, stop and comment on it. Encourage students to savor words. Talk about how the author chooses the very best words to "show" not just "tell." Contrast the "rich" word (elegant) with a "poor cousin" (good) word that the writer might have chosen, instead.

Students can collect their words in a notebook or file box. (See page xiv.) The words could also be posted on a word wall, organized either alphabetically or topically (e.g., Words That Describe Characters). Keep strips of construction paper handy so that you can write new words for the wall and post them as soon as they come up in reading or discussion. Encourage students to refer to the words when they are doing their own writing. You can use the words for games and activities such as word hunts.

Activities and Games

Frequent use and review helps students retain the meanings of new words. Activities and games can spark students' interest and make vocabulary acquisition fun. Use any or all of the following suggestions to help students learn and apply new vocabulary words, including the Enrichment Words.

Treasure Hunt

Ask students to collect examples of the vocabulary words in everyday use—on television or radio, in movies, in newspapers, novels, magazines, or in conversation. Students should write the sentences they find. Provide small strips of paper that can be stored in two different baskets, one for blank strips and one for completed strips. Once or twice a week, take the last ten minutes of a class for students to orally present their context sentences. If the sentences have been copied without errors, invite students to put them on display. (Give them a chance to correct any errors.) This simple activity can spark such great enthusiasm that you may end up with too many "treasures" to present in the time you have available! Students who did not present their findings can share their examples in groups and then put the examples on display.

Anything Goes

This game allows students to develop automaticity in word meaning and flexibility in response. Put a list of at least eight words, in any order, on the board, overhead transparency, or chart paper. Call on students individually and ask each one a question about a word. For example, ask one student to define a word, another to use a different word in a sentence, and a third to spell a derivative of a word (e.g., spell *spied* when the word on the board is *spy*). The task may be varied for different purposes; to focus on pronunciations, synonyms, or word parts, for example. You can award the class points for correct answers. Keep track of the points earned each day and compare with totals of other days.

Two in One

This game gives students practice in creating contexts for words. Challenge students to use two new words in one sentence, either orally or in writing. You may ask students to use any two words from a list, or you may make the game more challenging by asking students to use two specific words (or two of three words) in a sentence. Allow students to change the form of the words they use (by adding a suffix, for example). To facilitate creativity and discussion of words, have students work in groups.

Connect Two

List the words to be reviewed on the board, overhead transparency, or chart paper in two, three, or even four columns. Ask students to make a connection of any type between a word in one column and a word in another. Students may find similar meanings, categories (such as people, animals, pleasant words), common features, such as the same number of syllables or two words with suffixes, or some part of speech. Students may also make a connection by using two words from different columns in a sentence. You can limit the similarities to certain categories (meaning, structure) as you see fit.

Word Puzzles

Students can create an anagram or a crossword puzzle that uses all of the vocabulary words from a lesson or all the Enrichment Words from a unit.

Who Am I?

Have one student choose a word, such as Enrichment Word *brawny*, from Lesson 2, and write the word and its definition on an index card. The student can give two clues about the word. For example "I am an adjective. I describe strength." Class members then ask questions to try to identify the word. For example, "Do you describe people or objects? Are you positive or negative?" Small groups can form teams to play the game.

Choose the Right Words

Word choice is an important feature of effective writing. When students are revising, they should check to see that they have used the best words possible. For example, when talking about verbs, have students check all the action words in their current writing piece to see that they have used the most effective words. A helpful revision technique is for students to find a word with which they are not happy, circle it, and solicit class suggestions for replacement.

Dramatize the Words

The more involved students are with words, especially in a physical way, the better they will internalize them. Have students use movement to demonstrate a word. For example, in Lesson 2, students could step gingerly across the room, handle a fragile item, or draw an elaborate design.

Illustrate the Words

Students, especially visual learners, will benefit from illustrating words. In this book, words from Lessons 2–4 (words that describe characters and places), Lesson 9 (words with multiple meanings), and Lesson 24 (proverbs) are good candidates for illustration. Writing a description of a picture or labeling the illustration will extend the vocabulary concepts and make links to other words.

Word Sorts

Word sorts provide a physical way to work with the words. Have students make word cards for the selected vocabulary words and then place them in categories of their (open sort) or your (closed sort) choosing. Possible categories include related meaning, number of syllables, part of speech, and similar word part (prefix, suffix, root). Expand the categories by having students add other words that fit.

Word Web

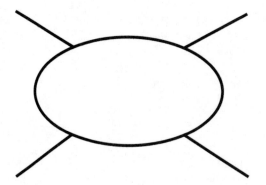

T-chart for _____

Rich Word Collection Sheet

Name _____

Date

Rich Word _____

I found this word in

_____

Name _____

Date

Rich Word _____

I found this word in

_____

Name _____

Date

Rich Word _____

I found this word in

_____

Name _____

Date

Rich Word _____

I found this word in

_____

Word List for Grade 5

abolish	45	discouraged	105	magnificent	25	Spartan (E)	92
academic	89	disgrace	105	maneuver (E)	32	species	49
acute	49	disintegrate (E)	108	marvel	29	spotless	5
ambidextrous (E)	116	dormant (E)	52	medium (E)	36	stealthily	25
ambition	113	drudge (E)	88	mentor	89	stubborn	85
amble	113	dusk	13	Midas touch	89	subculture (E)	68
amphibian	113	elaborate	5	mortal	53	submarine	65
appointed	45	elected	45	myth	53	submerged	65
apprentice	45	emaciated	5	nomad	25	subservient	65
arm	33	encircle	113	nimble (E)	28	subterranean	65
auditory	49	enclose	25	nutritious (E)	52	subzero	65
bicentennial	73	exquisite	5	observant	85	superabundant (E)	68
bilingual (E)	76	fate	53	odious	9	superfluous	65
biped	73	fearless	85	odyssey	89	superheated	65
brawny (E)	8	feast	29	olfactory	49	superimposed	65
candid (E)	12	fool	29	Olympian (E)	56	tactile	49
carriage	45	fragile	5	optimistic (E)	12	tattered	5
chaos (E)	92	frustrated	9	panic	89	timeless	53
charge	33	gloomy	13	plaza	13	transaction	109
circuitous	113	gorge	33	plea	25	transcontinental	109
circulate	113	guarantee	29	predator	49	transform	109
circumference	113	hamlet	13	proclamation (E)	48	transfusion	109
circumvent (E)	116	Herculean	89	prosperous	45	transition	109
colossal	89	homely	5	proverb	93	transitory (E)	112
commonplace	25	honorable	9	prying	85	translate	109
congested (E)	16	illegal	69	psyche	53	transplant	109
convene (E)	48	ill-informed	9	ravine	13	transport	109
counter (E)	36	illogical	69	realm	53	transpose (E)	112
cycle	113	immature	85	rebellion	45	triathlon (E)	76
dash	33	immodest	69	rebuke (E)	32	trilogy	73
deity (E)	56	immortal	53	reckless	85	triple	73
depression	33	immovable	69	representative	45	trivial	73
desperate	9	immune	69	responsive	49	unicellular	73
determined	85	imperfection	69	roam	25	unique	73
dilapidated (E)	16	impersonal (E)	72	roll	33	universe	73
din (E)	28	improper	69	ruefully	25	vegetation	13
disadvantage	105	intolerable	69	scholar (E)	88	vertebrate	49
disagreeable	105	invariably (E)	72	scout	29	vow	29
disaster	105	invincible	53	shiver	29	well-informed	9
discharge	105	lanky	5	shrewd	9	wrench	29
disclose (E)	108	lithe (E)	8	skeptical	89	yarn	33
discomfort	105	looming	13	skirt	33	youthful	85
discontent	105	lush	13	solemn	9		

(E) = Enrichment Words

Vocabulary Skills in *Vocabulary for Achievement*

	Grade 3	Grade 4	Grade 5
Analogies	Lessons 5, 10, 15, 20, 30	Lessons 5, 10, 15, 20, 25, 30	Lessons 5, 10, 15, 20, 25, 30
Antonyms	Lessons 1, 3, 5	Lessons 1, 2, 5, 10, 15	Lessons 10, 11, 15, 20, 25, 30
Compound Words	Lessons 1, 4	--	--
Connotations	--	--	Lessons 21, 22, 25, 30
Content-Area Words	Lessons 12, 13, 14, 15	Lessons 12, 13, 14, 15	Lessons 12, 13, 14, 15
Context	Lessons 5, 10, 11, 15, 20, 25	Lessons 5, 10, 11, 15, 20, 25, 30	Lessons 5, 10, 11, 12, 14, 15, 20, 25, 26, 30
Dictionary Skills	Lesson 6	Lessons 6, 11, 15	Lessons 6, 15, 21
Figurative Language	Lessons 21, 22, 24, 25	Lessons 21, 22	Lessons 24, 25
Homophones	Lessons 21, 23, 25	--	--
Multiple-Meaning Words	--	Lessons 6, 11, 15	Lessons 6, 8, 9, 10, 15
Parts of Speech	Lessons 6, 7, 8, 9, 10, 16, 18, 19, 20	Lessons 1, 3, 6, 7, 8, 9, 10, 16, 17, 18, 19	Lessons 1, 2, 3, 4, 6, 7, 8, 10, 15
Prefixes	Lessons 26, 27, 28, 29, 30	Lessons 26, 27, 28, 29, 30	Lessons 16, 17, 18, 19, 20, 26, 27, 28, 29, 30
Roots	Lessons 16, 17, 18, 26	Lessons 16, 17, 19, 20, 26, 30	Lessons 16, 17, 26, 27, 28, 29
Suffixes	Lessons 16, 17, 18, 19, 20	Lessons 16, 17, 18, 19, 20	Lessons 3, 16, 26
Synonyms	Lessons 1, 2, 3, 7, 8, 9, 12, 13, 15, 27, 28	Lessons 1, 4, 5, 8, 10, 13, 15, 29, 30	Lessons 1, 2, 5, 9, 10, 12, 14, 16, 18, 19, 20, 21, 25, 27, 30
Test-Taking Skills	Lessons 5, 10, 15, 20, 25, 30	Lessons 5, 10, 15, 20, 25, 30	Lessons 5, 10, 15, 20, 25, 30
Thesaurus Skills	--	Lesson 21	Lesson 21

VOCABULARY
for Achievement

Grade 5

Margaret Ann Richek

GREAT SOURCE
WILMINGTON, MA

Margaret Ann Richek

Professor, College of Education, Northeastern Illinois University; consultant in reading and vocabulary study; author of *The World of Words* (Houghton Mifflin)

Writing and Editing: Maryann Langen, Cara Lieb, Sue Paro

Text Design and Production: Publicom, Inc.

Illustrations: Rita Lascaro and Carol Maglitta

Cover Design: Publicom, Inc.

Cover Photo: Stone/Stuart Westmorland

Acknowledgments

The pronunciation key and the dictionary entries on pages 21-24 and 58-59: Copyright © 1998 by Houghton Mifflin Company. Reproduced by permission from THE AMERICAN HERITAGE CHILDREN'S DICTIONARY.

Thesaurus entries on pages 81 and 84: Copyright © 1997 by Paul Hellweg. Reproduced by permission from THE AMERICAN HERITAGE CHILDREN'S THESAURUS.

Printed in the United States

International Standard Book Number: 0-669-47128-3

1 2 3 4 5 6 7 8 9 10 - POO - 05 04 03 02 01 00

Contents

About This Book iv

PLAYING WITH WORDS

Lesson 1 . . . . .**SKILL LESSON:** synonyms **1**
Lesson 2 . . . . .To All Appearances: words about how things look **5**
Lesson 3 . . . . .In Character: words about people **9**
Lesson 4 . . . . .Picture This: words that tell about settings **13**
Lesson 5 . . . . .**REVIEW:** Lessons 1–4 . . . .**17**

WORKING WITH WORDS

Lesson 6 . . . . .**SKILL LESSON:** using the dictionary **21**
Lesson 7 . . . . .Just the Right Word: parts of speech **25**
Lesson 8 . . . . .Double Duty: words that are both nouns and verbs **29**
Lesson 9 . . . . .Same but Different: words with multiple meanings **33**
Lesson 10 . . . .**REVIEW:** Lessons 6–9 . . . .**37**

THINKING ABOUT WORDS

Lesson 11 . . . .**SKILL LESSON:** using context **41**
Lesson 12 . . . .Words for a New Nation: words from social studies . .**45**
Lesson 13 . . . .Making Sense: words from science **49**
Lesson 14 . . . .Traditional Tales: words from myths **53**
Lesson 15 . . . .**REVIEW:** Lessons 11–14 . . . .**57**

FORMING NEW WORDS

Lesson 16 . . . .**SKILL LESSON:** prefixes and suffixes **61**
Lesson 17 . . . .Under and Over: prefixes *sub-*, *super-* **65**
Lesson 18 . . . ."Not" Again!: prefixes *in-*, *il-*, *im-* **69**
Lesson 19 . . . .One, Two, Three . . . : prefixes *uni-*, *bi-*, *tri-* **73**
Lesson 20 . . . .**REVIEW:** Lessons 16–19 . . . .**77**

GOING BEYOND WORDS

Lesson 21 . . . .**SKILL LESSON:** using a thesaurus **81**
Lesson 22 . . . .Great Advice: proverbs **85**
Lesson 23 . . . .It's All Greek: words from Greek **89**
Lesson 24 . . . .Good or Bad?: shades of meaning **93**
Lesson 25 . . . .**REVIEW:** Lessons 21–24 . . . .**97**

LOOKING INTO WORDS

Lesson 26 . . . .**SKILL LESSON:** word parts **101**
Lesson 27 . . . .Opposite "Dis-": prefix *dis-* **105**
Lesson 28 . . . .Across the Way: prefix *trans-* **109**
Lesson 29 . . . .Around and Around: word parts *ambi-*, *amphi*, *circu-* **113**
Lesson 30 . . . .**REVIEW:** Lessons 26–29 . . . .**117**

Word List **121**

About This Book

That's a Lot of Words!

When you started school, you knew about 5,000 words. By the time you graduate from high school, you will probably know about 60,000 words! How does a person learn all those words? There are two main ways to learn new words: by reading a lot and by studying words.

You are in charge of reading a lot! However, in this book you will learn to study words by learning new words and meanings, understanding that words have different jobs to do (parts of speech), recognizing different forms of words, and using word parts.

Ways to Learn Words

A dictionary and a thesaurus will help you learn new words. For each word listed inside it, a **dictionary** tells the pronunciation, part of speech, and meaning(s). The pronunciation of a word helps you say the word. The part of speech tells whether a word is a noun, verb, adjective, or adverb. A word's definition describes what the word means and the ways it can be used. Sample sentences show you how the word can be used. For each word listed inside a **thesaurus,** there is a list of words that mean about the same thing, or synonyms. Use a thesaurus when you need a really clear, specific word in your writing.

This book will also teach you how to use synonyms, parts of speech and word parts to figure out words. Synonyms are words that mean the same thing as another word. Learning them helps you to use and understand different words. If you can figure out the part of speech of a word, it will help you understand what it means. Knowing the meanings of different word parts, such as prefixes, suffixes, and root words, can also help you figure out the meaning of unfamiliar words.

Be a Word Watcher

As you learn new words *in* this book, look for them *outside* the book. See if you can find the words in other books, newspapers, magazines, on TV, or even on the back of a cereal box. When you find a new word, share it with your class. Maybe you'll be the one to find the most new words this year. Good luck!

PLAYING WITH WORDS

Skill Lesson
synonyms, parts of speech

To write well, you need to be able to move words around, take some out, and put better ones in. In other words, you play with words. The next lessons in this book teach you ways to play with words, as well as describe appearances, personalities, and places.

dwelling   home   residence   house

 SYNONYMS A **synonym** is a word that means the same thing, or almost the same thing, as another word. When we use different synonyms, we change our words, and make our writing better. Read this paragraph and circle the word *nice* each time it is used.

> It was a nice day for a picnic. Aneisa had on her nice sun hat. Jason had packed a nice lunch for everybody. We all sat down on a nice blanket and enjoyed the nice weather. When the picnic was over, we all played a nice game of soccer.

Use the pictures on pages 1 and 2 to help introduce or review synonyms.

You can make the writing more interesting by replacing *nice* with synonyms. Choose the synonym that works best in each sentence below and write it on the line.

Lesson 1 introduces and practices skills that students will use in Lessons 2–4.

It was a **(1)** _____pleasant_____ *(sweet/pleasant)* day for a picnic. Aneisa had on her **(2)** _____beautiful_____ *(beautiful/friendly)* sun hat. Jason had packed a **(3)** _____delicious_____ *(fun/delicious)* lunch for everybody. We all sat down on a **(4)** _____cozy_____ *(cozy/polite)* blanket and had a **(5)** _____friendly_____ *(friendly/tasty)* talk. When the picnic was over, we all played a **(6)** _____fun_____ *(beautiful/fun)* game of soccer.

USING SYNONYMS Now try this example, using synonyms for the word *go*. Choose the word that works best in each sentence and write it on the line.

The girls decided to **(1)** _____ hike _____ *(hike/stroll)* up the mountain. Mindy wanted to **(2)** _____ race _____ *(race/continue)* as fast as she could, while Dara preferred to **(3)** _____ stroll _____ *(stroll/race)* more slowly. The two girls worked hard to **(4)** _____ climb _____ *(run/climb)* all the way to the top. After their hard work, the girls took the time to **(5)** _____ walk _____ *(march/walk)* around the top to look at the view.

Below are lists of synonyms. Add a synonym of your own that fits with each list. Share your words with a partner.

6. run, hurry, _____ (race, scurry, jog) _____

7. kneel, bend, _____ (crouch, stoop) _____

8. kick, knock, _____ (hit, tap, boot) _____

9. haul, drag, _____ (pull, tow, tug) _____

10. kind, gentle, _____ (nice, helpful, thoughtful) _____

11. big, immense, _____ (large, gigantic, enormous) _____

12. silly, comical, _____ (crazy, foolish, funny) _____

13. quiet, hushed, _____ (still, silent, peaceful) _____

14. brilliant, bright, _____ (smart, intelligent) _____

15. throw, fling, _____ (toss, pitch, hurl) _____

Sharing their words is the best way for students to become exposed to more words than they can think of on their own.

C **PARTS OF SPEECH** The part of speech, or the way a word works in a sentence, helps you to understand and use a word. Each word in this book is listed with its part of speech. Let's review some parts of speech now.

A **noun** is a person, animal, place, thing, or idea.

Examples: My brother (person) told me his plan (idea) for making money (thing).

Roberto (person) walked his dog (animal) in the park (place).

An **adjective** describes a noun.

Examples: Daryl is a likeable boy with an easy manner.

The busy crew worked quickly to clean the dirty warehouse.

A **verb** is a word for an action or way of being.

Examples: The earth spins on its axis as it orbits the sun (action).
Anna is tall for her age. (way of being).

An **adverb** describes a verb.

Examples: I will gladly pay you for these yummy muffins!

The tornado moved slowly across the countryside.

Circle the part of speech of the word in dark type.

1. The Mayan Indians **built** many pyramids.   noun / (verb)

2. Samuel is a **great** carpenter.   adverb / (adjective)

3. The student responded **slowly** to the principal's questions.
(adverb) / verb

4. Yesterday was the first day of our **vacation**.   (noun) / adjective

Ask students to draw arrows from the adjectives to the nouns they describe. Likewise, have them connect the adverbs to the verbs.

ADJECTIVES Adjectives are words that describe or tell about something. Start a collection of adjectives to use in your writing. Fill in the categories below.

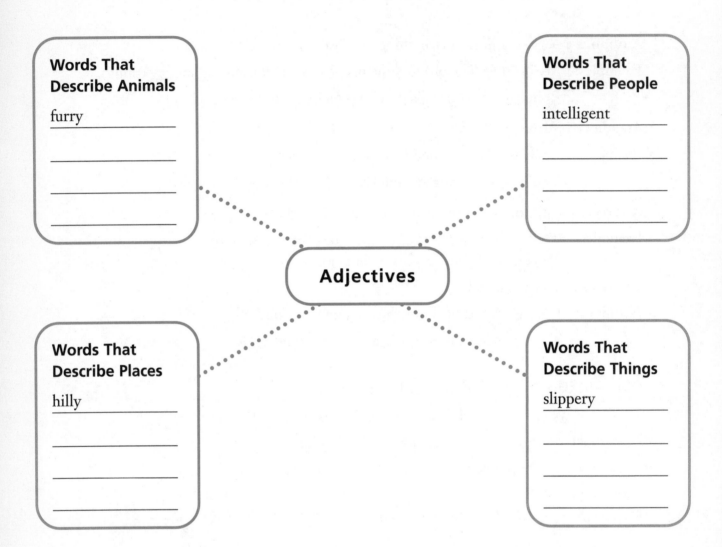

Words That Describe Animals

furry

_____

_____

Words That Describe People

intelligent

_____

_____

_____

Adjectives

Words That Describe Places

hilly

_____

_____

_____

Words That Describe Things

slippery

_____

_____

_____

The power of this exercise is in having students share their words, building on each other's ideas. To collect everyone's words, keep a word file, notebook, or word wall of adjectives.

Point out that students are asked to think of adjectives that describe four of the kinds of nouns mentioned on page 3.

LESSON 2

To All Appearances
words about how things look

A Are you sometimes at a loss for words when you try to describe something you have seen? The words below all describe appearances, or how things look. All the words are adjectives.

a tattered flag

Ask students to choose an object in the room and brainstorm all the words they can think of to describe how it looks. Review "words that describe," or adjectives. Then go over the introduction and words with students.

1. **elaborate** (ĭ lăb' ər ĭt)
*Something **elaborate** is complicated and has lots of parts or details.* (adjective)
The **elaborate** birthday cake has seven layers and three fruit fillings.

2. **emaciated** (ĭ mā' shē āt' ĭd)
*An **emaciated** person or animal is very thin from starvation.* (adjective)
The cows were so **emaciated** that we could see the outlines of their ribs.

3. **exquisite** (ĕk' skwĭz ĭt)
*Something **exquisite** is very beautiful and fine.* (adjective)
The **exquisite** box was covered with jewels and tiny gold patterns.

4. **fragile** (frăj' əl)
*Something or someone **fragile** is easily broken or hurt.* (adjective)
The **fragile** crystal glasses broke when they bumped together.

5. **homely** (hōm' lē)
*A **homely** person is ugly or not attractive.* (adjective)
The **homely** baby grew to be a cute little child.

6. **lanky** (lăng' kē)
*A **lanky** person is tall and thin.* (adjective)
The **lanky** teenager was fondly nicknamed "Stringbean."

7. **spotless** (spŏt' lĭs)
*Something **spotless** is very clean.* (adjective)
The **spotless** restaurant kitchen passed the state inspection easily.

8. **tattered** (tăt' ərd)
*Something that is **tattered** is torn, old, and ragged. Tattered often refers to cloth.* (adjective)
The **tattered** flag in the museum had been carried in many battles.

Draw a line between each word and its synonym.

1. fragile — breakable
2. emaciated — skinny
3. tattered — raggedy
4. elaborate — detailed

© Great Source DO NOT COPY

B All the boldfaced words in the passage below tell about appearances in some way. Read the passage. Then answer the questions that follow.

An Aesop's Fable: Don't Count Your Chickens

One summer day long ago, a young woman walked to town, carrying a pail of milk on her head. As she went along, she said to herself, "I have worked hard, but now I can plan my future. When I get to town, I will sell this milk, take the money, and buy a hen. The hen will lay eggs, and I will protect them carefully, because eggs are **fragile.** After the chicks are born, I will feed them well so they won't become **emaciated.** When they are healthy chickens, I can sell them. Soon I will have lots of money. This dress is stained and **tattered.** I will throw it away and buy an **exquisite** new one with lovely bows and ribbons. I'll save it for the first big party in town so it will be **spotless.**

"When I get to the party, all the young men will ask me to dance. But I will choose only the strongest and most handsome. I don't want to dance with anyone who is too tall and **lanky.** And if somebody **homely** asks me, I shall shake my head and say, 'No!'"

The milkmaid tossed her head in the air, and the pail tumbled to the ground, spilling milk all over her. That was the end of the young woman's **elaborate** plans.

The lesson we can learn from this is "Don't count your chickens until they are hatched!"

1. Is the young woman rich or poor? How can you tell?

   She is probably poor because she makes plans to earn money. Her dress is

   tattered and stained.

2. What makes the young woman's plans elaborate?

   Her plans depend on many different things. She has to sell the milk and buy

   hens. Then the hens have to lay eggs, and the chicks have to grow up so the

   woman can sell them.

Name

Date

elaborate

emaciated

exquisite

fragile

homely

lanky

spotless

tattered

C Choose the word from the two choices given that best fits in each sentence. Write the word on the line.

1. My favorite old jeans are _____tattered_____ and torn. *(exquisite/tattered)*

2. Dad wiped the kitchen counter until it was _____spotless_____. *(lanky/spotless)*

3. The wind ripped through the _____fragile_____ paper kite. *(fragile/emaciated)*

4. The _____elaborate_____ rules of the computer game are very difficult to master. *(tattered/elaborate)*

5. When the supply of food runs out, people may become _____emaciated_____. *(emaciated/homely)*

D The sentences below can be made more descriptive if you provide a **synonym** to replace the underlined word or words. Write a word from the word list on each line that means about the same as the underlined word(s). Notice that sometimes you will replace two words with one word.

1. A medical laboratory needs to be <u>very clean</u>. _____spotless_____

2. Something <u>easily breakable</u> must be wrapped carefully. _____fragile_____

3. Some people think that bulldogs are <u>ugly</u>, but I think they're cute. _____homely_____

4. We made <u>complicated</u> plans to get all 100 children to the picnic. _____elaborate_____

5. The small painting had <u>very fine</u> detail. _____exquisite_____

6. Our <u>tall, thin</u> friend towered above us. _____lanky_____

7. Alicia took the <u>torn, old</u> shirt and made it into a rag. _____tattered_____

8. We felt sorry for the <u>very thin</u> people who couldn't get food after the flood. _____emaciated_____

Review that synonyms are words that mean about the same.

OTHER FORMS

elaborately

exquisitely

fragility

spotlessly

 Complete each sentence with a word or phrase that makes sense. Some other forms of the vocabulary words are used.

1. You might wear **tattered** clothes to _____ .

2. An **exquisitely** dressed person might be wearing _____

   _____ .

3. **Elaborate** directions can be _____ .

4. A **fragile** vase _____ .

5. If something shines **spotlessly,** it _____

   _____ .

Point out that with different endings, words become different parts of speech. By adding *ly* to *spotless,* you have *spotlessly,* an adverb that tells how something is done. Note that adverb forms of the words are used in exercise E.

ENRICHMENT WORDS

Here are two more words that you can use to describe appearances.

1. brawny (brô' nē) *Someone who is* **brawny** *has well-developed muscles and is strong.* (adjective)

   The **brawny** man lifted weights every day.

2. lithe (līth) *Someone who is* **lithe** *moves gracefully.* (adjective)

   The **lithe** gymnast performed a graceful routine on the balance beam.

See page viii for Enrichment Word activities.

OFF THE PAGE

Make a chart like the one shown here for at least one of the other words in this lesson. Use the example of *fragile* as a guide.

Off the Page activities can be done in class or as homework.

Things That Are Fragile	Synonyms for Fragile
Glass	Breakable
Butterflies	Delicate
Taco shells	
Old paper	

LESSON 3

In Character
words about people

happy funny smart young

A The words below all describe a person's character. Think about times you have seen a person be, for example, honorable, shrewd, or frustrated.

1. **desperate** (dĕs' pər ĭt) *To be* **desperate** *is to need or want something so much that you are almost hopeless.* (adjective)
The **desperate** man reached out for the lifeboat to keep from drowning.

2. **frustrated** (frŭs' trā təd) *To be* **frustrated** *is to be discouraged or prevented from reaching a goal.* (adjective)
Mom was **frustrated** in her effort to keep the kitchen floor clean because the baby kept dropping his food.

3. **honorable** (ŏn' ər ə bəl) *An* **honorable** *person has high moral standards and deserves respect.* (adjective)
Cheating on tests is not **honorable** behavior.

4. **ill-informed** (ĭl' ĭn fôrmd') *Someone who is* **ill-informed** *does not have enough information or has the wrong information.* (adjective)
An **ill-informed** citizen will not know how to vote in an election.

5. **odious** (ō' dē əs) *An* **odious** *person or thing causes or deserves hate.* (adjective)
The **odious** ruler put thousands of people in prison.

6. **shrewd** (shrōōd) *A* **shrewd** *person is clever in useful ways.* (adjective)
A **shrewd** shopper watches the newspapers for sales.

7. **solemn** (sŏl' əm) *To be* **solemn** *is to be serious or grave in manner.* (adjective)
The doctor gave us the bad news with a **solemn** voice.

8. **well-informed** (wĕl' ĭn fôrmd') *Someone who is* **well-informed** *has accurate information.* (adjective)
The school's Web site keeps parents **well-informed** about homework.

Draw a line between each word and its synonym.
1. frustrated   hopeless
2. shrewd   good
3. desperate   clever
4. honorable   prevented

Have students do a quickwrite to answer this question: "If someone were to describe you, what words would you like them to use?" As students share their responses, point out that some words have good meanings and others have negative meanings.

All the boldfaced words in the passage below tell about character in some way. Read the passage and answer the questions.

Benjamin O. Davis: Leader of the Tuskegee Airmen

Retired General Benjamin O. Davis looked very **solemn** on the day he was promoted to four-star general. He may have been thinking about his long battle against racial discrimination in the Army. When Davis entered West Point in 1932, he faced constant prejudice there. In an **odious** attempt to make him quit, other students gave him "the silent treatment," refusing to talk to him for four years. Davis was **shrewd** enough to realize that complaints would only bring more trouble. He refused to be **frustrated** in achieving his goals. Instead, he studied hard and graduated near the top of his class.

Davis was **desperate** to be a pilot, but he was rejected until World War II broke out. Many **ill-informed** white officers believed African Americans were not smart enough to fly or brave enough to fight. They were soon proved to be wrong. During World War II, African Americans were trained as pilots at the Tuskegee Institute. In combat, commanded by Davis, the Tuskegee Airmen achieved one of the best records of World War II. Davis's unit shot down more than 200 enemy aircraft. The American bomber crews, **well-informed** about the expertise of the Tuskegee Airmen, nicknamed them "Red-Tail Angels" because the tails of their planes were painted bright red. Not a single American bomber plane protected by Davis's 332nd Fighter Group was ever shot down.

Their outstanding performance was an important reason that the armed forces were integrated shortly after World War II. Davis became a three-star general. Fourteen years after he retired, he was awarded a fourth star because of his **honorable** service in the U.S. Army.

WORD LIST

desperate

frustrated

honorable

ill-informed

odious

shrewd

solemn

well-informed

1. What problem did Benjamin O. Davis encounter at West Point? Use a word from the word list to describe the people who caused this problem.

   Students should show an understanding of the word(s) they use.

2. Choose a boldfaced word from the passage that best describes Davis. Explain your choice.

   Answers will vary.

C Choose the word from the two choices given that best fits in each sentence. Write the word on the line.

1. When you break something, the *(frustrated/honorable)* thing to do is admit it. ___honorable___

2. A graduation is a *(desperate/solemn)*, but happy, occasion. ___solemn___

3. Destroying property is *(odious/well-informed)* behavior. ___odious___

4. The art dealer gave me a *(shrewd/honorable)* look when he offered me only $20 for the fine painting. ___shrewd___

5. The mother bear climbed over the fence, *(well-informed/desperate)* to get food for her cubs. ___desperate___

D Adding *-ly* to a word makes it an adverb. An adverb describes how something is done or how someone behaves. For example, *desperately* describes someone who behaves in a desperate way. When a word ends in *le*, the *l* and *e* are dropped before *-ly* is added. Use number 1 as a model to fill in the blanks below.

1. desperately   = desperate   + ly = in a desperate way

2. shrewdly   = ___shrewd___   + ly = ___in a shrewd way___

3. odiously   = ___odious___   + ly = ___in an odious way___

4. honorably   = ___honorable___ + ly = ___in an honorable way___

5. solemnly   = ___solemn___   + ly = ___in a solemn way___

Review that looking at word parts can help understand new words. Have students suggest other adverbs that end in *-ly*.

OTHER FORMS
desperately
desperation
frustration
odiously
shrewdly
honorably
solemnly

E Complete each sentence with a phrase that makes sense. Note that some other forms of the vocabulary words are used in the sentences.

1. People feel **frustration** when _____

_____ .

2. An example of a **solemn** occasion is _____

_____ .

3. Olivia was **ill-informed** about the weather, so she _____

_____ .

4. A **shrewd** judge of character _____

_____ .

5. Someone who behaves **honorably** _____

_____ .

Show how different forms of a word do different jobs in sentences: The *desperate* man stole food from a sidewalk vendor. The man wanted *desperately* to eat.

ENRICHMENT WORDS

Here are two more words that can be used to describe someone's character. Have you seen these words before?

See page viii for Enrichment Word activities.

1. **candid** (kăn' dĭd) *A* **candid** *person is open and honest in expressing opinions.* (adjective)
   When Dad gave his **candid** opinion of my paper, I decided to rewrite it.

2. **optimistic** (ŏp' tə mĭs' tĭk) *An* **optimistic** *person views things in the most hopeful and positive way.* (adjective)
   Sue thought she had failed the test, but her mother was more **optimistic**.

optimistic

OFF THE PAGE

Think of a character in a book that you have read. Use one or more of the vocabulary words to describe this character. For example: In the book *Shiloh* by Phyllis Reynolds Naylor, Shiloh's owner could be described as **odious** because he mistreats dogs.

Picture This
words that tell about setting

A Settings help us to imagine where a story takes place. An adventure story might take place on a lonely mountain or a stormy sea. A science-fiction story might be in outer space. The words below help you to describe settings when you write and to understand them when you read.

lush vegetation

1. **dusk** (dŭsk) **Dusk** *is the time of evening just before darkness.* (noun)
Many state forests close at **dusk** because the woods are dangerous after dark.

2. **gloomy** (gloo' mē) *A* **gloomy** *place is darkened, without much light; a* **gloomy** *person is sad.* (adjective)
Heavy, closed curtains made the room look **gloomy** even on a sunny day.

3. **hamlet** (hăm' lĭt) *A* **hamlet** *is a small town or village.* (noun)
One Indiana **hamlet** has the unusual name of Gnaw Bone.

4. **looming** (loom' ĭng) *Something that is* **looming** *appears to be large and frightening.* (verb)
Tall, dark cliffs were **looming** above us as we pulled our boat to shore.

5. **lush** (lŭsh) *Something* **lush** *is filled with thick, healthy, plentiful plant life.* (adjective)
The rain forests of Hawaii are a **lush** mix of flowers, shrubs, and trees.

6. **plaza** (plăz' ə) *A* **plaza** *is a public square in a town or city or a shopping center.* (noun)
Summer concerts are held on the **plaza** at the center of town.

7. **ravine** (rə vēn') *A* **ravine** *is a deep, narrow gorge or valley.* (noun)
Engineers designed a bridge that crossed the **ravine.**

8. **vegetation** (vĕj' ĭ tā' shən)
Vegetation *is plant life.* (noun)
Prairie grass and other natural **vegetation** grow on the Great Plains.

Draw a line between the word and its definition.

1. lush — dark or sad
2. gloomy — early evening
3. vegetation — plentiful
4. dusk — plant life

Choose a book that the class has read. Ask students to describe the setting—the place, the time. Make a list of descriptive words and phrases. Compare the list with the new words, which all tell about settings.

B All the boldfaced words in the passage below tell about settings in some way. Read the passage and answer the questions.

The Day the Mountain Blew Its Top

In April, 1980, Mount St. Helens volcano had been "sleeping" for more than a hundred years. Its slopes were covered with trees, wildflowers, and other **vegetation.** The mountain was home to birds, bears, elk, and deer. It was a popular recreation area for hikers, boaters, and nature lovers. But on May 18, 1980, the sleeping volcano suddenly awakened and blew its top.

The blast tore the top off the mountain and flattened the tall fir forests on its slopes. Avalanches swept down the mountain, pouring rock, dirt, and mud into the valleys and **ravines** below.

Meanwhile, a huge column of ash and gas was **looming** over the mountain. It was only noon, but it looked like **dusk.** The ash made the sky so dark and **gloomy** that in a small **hamlet** 80 miles away, the streetlights came on in the middle of the day. The ash fell like rain on the shopping **plazas,** houses, streets, and cars of nearby towns.

Back on the mountain, everything had changed. The **lush** forests were gone. The animals were gone. The slopes were now covered with a thick, gray layer of rock and ash. It looked dead. Just a few years later, life began to return to Mount St. Helens. Scientists have been amazed to see how quickly seeds have sprouted, plants have grown, and animals have begun to return.

WORD LIST

dusk

gloomy

hamlet

looming

lush

plaza

ravine

vegetation

1. Why did the streetlights come on in a small hamlet 80 miles away? Use at least two of the boldfaced words in your answer. _____

   The ash covered the sun, making the sky so gloomy that it looked like dusk.

   _____

2. List two types of vegetation from the passage. _____

   Trees and wildflowers are mentioned in the passage.

   _____

C Find the words in the word list that fit each description.

1. Write a word (a noun) that tells a time of the day. _____ *dusk* _____

2. Write three words (nouns) that name places. _____

   hamlet, plaza, ravine

3. Write three words (adjectives) that describe how something looks.

   gloomy, looming, lush

D Remember that using **synonyms** can make your writing more interesting. Use the words from the word list as synonyms for the underlined word or words below. Remember that you can replace more than one word with a single word.

As I walked through the (1) <u>thick</u> forest, I saw the (2) <u>little town</u> in the distance. At (3) <u>the time of day when the sun was setting</u>, I began to make out the (4) <u>public square</u> and the people carrying umbrellas on the (5) <u>dark and dreary</u> day.

1. _____ *lush* _____
2. _____ *hamlet* _____
3. _____ *dusk* _____
4. _____ *plaza* _____
5. _____ *gloomy* _____

E Complete each sentence with a phrase that makes sense. Some other forms of the vocabulary words have been used.

1. **Dusk** is a good time for _____ .

2. A **gloomy** day is _____ .

3. Two huge trees **loom** over _____ .

4. If the **vegetation** is growing **lushly,** _____

_____ .

5. Living in a **hamlet** would be _____

because _____ .

Remind students that when they know one word, they can easily learn many others. For example, *gloom, gloomy, gloomily.*

ENRICHMENT WORDS

Here are two more words that can be used to describe a setting.

1. **congested** (kən **jĕs**' tĭd) *To be* **congested** *is to be overcrowded.*
   (adjective)
   The road became **congested** because construction crews closed a lane.

2. **dilapidated** (dĭ **lăp**' ĭ dā' tĭd) *Something that is* **dilapidated** *is in bad condition and needs repair.* (adjective)
   The **dilapidated** house had broken windows and peeling paint.

See page viii for Enrichment Word activities.

OFF THE PAGE

The details you put in your writing help the reader "see" what you are writing about. Choose one of the settings below. Help your readers "see" the setting by using at least three details in a paragraph to describe it. One detail might be: *All the colors turned to gray as dusk fell on the hamlet.*

1. a hamlet at dusk

2. a gloomy mansion

3. a lush forest

a gloomy mansion

Review
Lessons 1-4

In this lesson, you will review the words and strategies
you have learned in the last four lessons. This will help
you to remember them when you read and write.

 A **MATCHING WORDS AND DEFINITIONS**
Choose the word that matches each definition. Write it on the line.

| gloomy | tattered | homely | shrewd | vegetation |

1. darkened or sad _____gloomy_____

2. torn, old, and ragged _____tattered_____

3. grasses and flowers _____vegetation_____

4. clever _____shrewd_____

5. unattractive, ugly _____homely_____

B **USING WORDS IN CONTEXT**
Use the words in each list to complete each paragraph.

| desperate | dusk | odious | homely | solemn |

As the sun lowered and **(1)** _____dusk_____ approached, Jonathan
became more nervous. He was **(2)** _____desperate_____ to finish breaking
the code before the morning. Bored and annoyed by the **(3)** _____odious_____
task, he scribbled out draft after draft of the mysterious coded message.
He wrote continuously until his arm ached. Finally, just before dawn, he
discovered the key and decoded the letter.

| plaza | looming | ravine | exquisite | solemn |

Adam hiked down the steep **(4)** _____ravine_____ as the rain fell.
Then he saw it. Under a broad leaf were some ancient bones. Next
to them was an **(5)** _____exquisite_____ necklace of sparkling stones.
He carefully picked it up and took a closer look. His expression became
(6) _____solemn_____ when he realized the importance of his discovery.

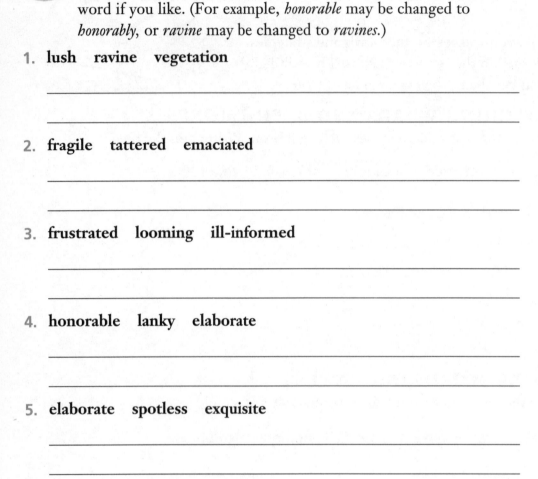

C **WRITING SENTENCES** Choose two of the words on each line to use in a sentence. You can change the form of the word if you like. (For example, *honorable* may be changed to *honorably*, or *ravine* may be changed to *ravines*.)

1. **lush   ravine   vegetation**

   _____

   _____

2. **fragile   tattered   emaciated**

   _____

   _____

3. **frustrated   looming   ill-informed**

   _____

   _____

4. **honorable   lanky   elaborate**

   _____

   _____

5. **elaborate   spotless   exquisite**

   _____

   _____

D **TEST-TAKING STRATEGIES** An **analogy** compares word pairs that are related in some way. An analogy can be expressed in a sentence like the one here.

If students have little or no experience with analogies, model how to solve an analogy by thinking out loud.

Scared is to frightened as tired is to sleepy.

Strategy: To complete an analogy, find out how the words in the first pair are related. The second pair must have the same relationship. *Scared* means about the same as *frightened*, and *tired* means about the same as *sleepy*. Both pairs of words are synonyms. Some analogies are "type of" analogies. For example: A dog is a type of animal, and a maple is a type of tree. The analogy is "Dog is to animal as maple is to tree."

Directions: Choose the word that completes each analogy and write it on the line.

1. Dirty is to filthy as spotless is to _____clean_____. *(soap/clean)*

2. Small is to tiny as ripped is to _____tattered_____. *(tattered/little)*

3. Large is to huge as dark is to _____gloomy_____. *(bright/gloomy)*

4. Honest is to truthful as solemn is to _____serious_____. *(serious/silent)*

5. Pretty is to beautiful as unattractive is to _____homely_____. *(lovely/homely)*

6. House is to building as hamlet is to _____town_____. *(town/garage)*

7. Lush is to adjective as vegetation is to _____noun_____. *(adverb/noun)*

8. Lobby is to indoor space as plaza is to _____outdoor space_____. *(outdoor space/hotel)*

9. Piano is to instrument as grass is to _____vegetation_____. *(flowers/vegetation)*

10. Honorable is to adjective as ravine is to _____noun_____. *(verb/noun)*

> Model how to determine the word relationships. For example, "Dirty means the same as filthy. What means the same as spotless?"

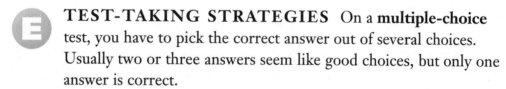 **TEST-TAKING STRATEGIES** On a **multiple-choice** test, you have to pick the correct answer out of several choices. Usually two or three answers seem like good choices, but only one answer is correct.

Strategy: Read through each question. Before you search for an answer, think of how you would answer the question. Then look to see if your answer is there. If it is and you are certain it is correct, carefully fill in the bubble next to the answer. If your answer is not there, find the answers that you know are *not* correct. Skip them and focus on the remaining choices. When you decide on your answer, fill in the bubble completely.

Directions: Fill in the bubble next to the word that answers the question.

1. What is another word for *gloomy?*

   (A) nervous   (B) sad   (C) tired   (D) thin

2. How would you describe a tiny, hand-blown glass swan knick-knack?

   (A) lanky   (B) lush   (C) fragile   (D) gloomy

3. What word means about the same as *shrewd?*

   (A) clever   (B) stubborn   (C) sneaky   (D) solemn

4. Which of the following is most likely to be well-informed about high-quality clothing?

   (A) fashion designer   (B) insurance salesperson

   (C) waiter or waitress   (D) doctor or nurse

5. What is another way of saying that someone is extremely thin?

   (A) shrewd   (B) honorable

   (C) exquisite   (D) emaciated

See page 125 for a reproducible test in standardized-test format.

ENRICHMENT WORDS

Draw a line between each Enrichment Word and its definition.

1. brawny — graceful
2. lithe — overcrowded, overfilled
3. optimistic — bad condition, needs repair
4. candid — having muscles, fit
5. dilapidated — seeing things in a good light
6. congested — open and honest

LESSON 6

WORKING WITH WORDS

Skill Lesson
Using the Dictionary

The **dictionary** is a good tool to help you improve your vocabulary. It can help you learn new words and understand the many shades of meaning of words you may already know. It can also help you pronounce words correctly.

A **DICTIONARY ENTRIES** People who write dictionaries give a lot of information in a small space. They use shortcuts and abbreviations to keep things brief. The information given for a word in the dictionary is called an **entry.** Look at the entry below.

> ┌─1──────┐ ┌─2─┐┌──3──────────────┐
> **grandfather** *noun* The father of one's father or mother.
> **grand•fa•ther (grand' fä'thər)** Δ *noun, plural* **grandfathers**
>   └─4─┘   └─5─┘

Compare this style with that of your classroom dictionary. Note similarities and differences.

1. **The word.** The entry word is printed in boldface type.

2. **The part of speech.** The part of speech is printed in italic type.

3. **The definition.** This tells what the word means. If there is more than one definition, each will be numbered.

4. **Syllables and pronunciation.** A key shows how to use the symbols. A small mark (') shows which syllable to stress.

5. **Other forms.** Other forms of the word that do not have their own entries may be listed here. The parts of speech may also be included.

This dictionary entry has example sentences. Answer the questions.

> **pretend** *verb* **1.** To put on a false show of: *They pretended illness.*
> **2.** To make believe: *Let's pretend we're famous.*
> **pre•tend (prĭ tĕnd')** Δ *verb* **pretended, pretending**

1. What part of speech is *pretend*? _____verb_____

2. How many syllables are in *pretend*? _____two_____

3. How many definitions are there of *pretend*? _____2_____

4. Which syllable is the accented syllable in *pretend*? ___the second: tend___

B **PARTS OF SPEECH** Some words can be different **parts of speech**, depending on how they are used. For example, the word *farm* can be a place (noun) as well as an action (verb). Here is what the dictionary entry for *farm* looks like:

> **farm** *noun* **1.** A piece of land on which crops or animals are raised. Δ *verb* **1.** To engage in farming. **2.** To cultivate or produce a crop on **farm** (färm) Δ *noun, plural* **farms** Δ *verb* **farmed, farming**

This sentence shows *farm* used as a **noun.**

My mother lived on a **farm** when she was a little girl.

This sentence shows *farm* used as a **verb.**

In the coming season, the Swansons decided to **farm** rice and beans on their land.

In the dictionary entry below, sample sentences help you understand *promise*.

farm

> **promise** *noun* **1.** A statement that one will do something; vow: *I kept my promise to write home.*
> **2.** Reason for expecting something, such as future success, excellence, or distinction: *The young dancer shows promise.* Δ *verb* **1.** To make a promise: *I promised to come home early.* **2.** To give reasons for expecting: *The dark clouds promised rain.*
> **prom•ise** (prŏm' ĭs) Δ *noun, plural* **promises** Δ *verb* **promised, promising**

Review parts of speech as necessary for your students. Lesson 8 is about words that are both nouns and verbs.

How is the word *promise* used in the following sentences? Write *noun* or *verb* on the line.

1. I **promise** to be at the club meeting tomorrow—no matter what!
   _____verb_____

2. We can be friends only if you **promise** never to do that again.
   _____verb_____

3. A **promise** is a **promise.** _____noun_____

4. We can still keep our **promise** and help clean up. _____noun_____

5. You made a **promise** to me that I will never forget. _____noun_____

C **MULTIPLE-MEANING WORDS** Some words have two or more meanings that are quite different from each other. These different meanings can be the same part of speech, or they can be different parts of speech. These kinds of words are called **multiple-meaning words.** For example, the word *trunk* can refer to part of a tree, an elephant, or a car. It can also be a large box.

Here is a dictionary entry for the multiple-meaning word *coach*. Use the entry to fill in the blanks below.

Remind students to use the context of the sentence to figure out which meaning of a word is meant. Lesson 9 is on multiple-meaning words.

> **coach** *noun* **1.** A large carriage with four wheels that has seats inside and is drawn by horses. **2.** A person who trains or teaches athletes, athletic teams, or performers.
> **coach** (kōch) Δ *noun, plural* **coaches**

Read each sentence and decide how the word *coach* is used. Write the number of the correct definition on the line in front of each sentence.

1. ___1___ The passenger jumped into the **coach** and away they rode.
2. ___2___ Daisy couldn't help smiling at her **coach** after the big win.
3. ___1___ After the **coach** pulled into town, the driver fed and watered the horses.
4. ___2___ "We did our best and that's what counts," said the **coach.**
5. ___1___ The king and queen waved from the royal **coach.**

Read the dictionary entry for *cow* and answer the questions below.

> **cow** *noun* **1.** The fully grown female of cattle, raised for its milk, meat, and hide. **2.** The female of certain other large mammals, as the elephant. Δ *verb* To frighten with threats.
> **cow** (kou) Δ *noun, plural* **cows** Δ *verb* **cowed**

6. Which noun definition of *cow* is used in the following sentence?

   The walrus **cow** pulled herself out of the water. _____2_____

7. Which noun definition of *cow* is used in the following sentence?

   The **cows** entered the barn at milking time. _____1_____

8. Which part of speech is *cow* in the following sentence?

   The cruel giant **cowed** David with an angry stare.

   _____verb_____

9. What part of speech is *cow* in the following sentence?

   Of all our **cows**, Bessy was my father's favorite. _____noun, plural_____

COWS

Just the Right Word
different parts of speech

apples   red   easily

pick

A In Lesson 1, you learned about parts of speech. In Lesson 6, you saw how they function in dictionary entries. This lesson will help you to review parts of speech by teaching you two new nouns, verbs, adjectives, and adverbs.

1. **commonplace** (kŏm' ən plās')
Something **commonplace** *is ordinary and uninteresting.* (adjective)
A clover with three leaves is **commonplace,** but a four-leaf clover is very unusual.

2. **enclose** (ĕn klōz') To **enclose** *means to put something in a closed place.* (verb)
My aunt likes to **enclose** money in my birthday card.

3. **magnificent** (măg nĭf' ĭ sənt)
Something **magnificent** *is excellent or wonderful.* (adjective)
Mark McGwire and Sammy Sosa have **magnificent** home run records.

4. **nomad** (nō' măd') *A* **nomad** *is a person who moves from place to place in search of food.* (noun)
A **nomad** who raises cattle in the Himalayas lives in a round tent called a *yurt.*

5. **plea** (plē) *A* **plea** *is an urgent request or call for help.* (noun)
The governor made a special **plea** to the president to provide emergency flood aid.

6. **roam** (rōm) *When we* **roam,** *we wander, or travel around from place to place without a plan.* (verb)
My parents don't allow me to **roam** around the mall by myself.

7. **ruefully** (rōo' fəl ē) **Ruefully** *means done with regret or sorrow.* (adverb) "I wish I hadn't climbed that tree," Lin said **ruefully,** as she rubbed her sprained ankle.

8. **stealthily** (stĕlth' ĭ lē) **Stealthily** *means done in a quiet, secret manner.* (adverb)
The six-year old child **stealthily** opened the cabinet and reached for the cookies.

Review the name and function of the four common parts of speech. Next have students list four words for each part of speech. Finally, have students put the words together in sentences that have the following format:
The _____ (adjective) _____ (noun) _____ (verb) _____ (adverb).

Draw a line between each vocabulary word and its synonym.

1. nomad   request
2. plea   wonderful
3. magnificent   ordinary
4. roam   travel
5. commonplace   wanderer

B All the boldfaced words in the passage below are either nouns, verbs, adverbs, or adjectives. Read the passage. Then answer the questions that follow.

The Nightingale: A Hans Christian Andersen Story

Long ago, an emperor lived in a **magnificent** palace. Visitors wrote of his great riches, but what they praised most about the country was the sweet song of a plain little gray bird, a nightingale. Curious, the emperor had the nightingale brought to him.

When he heard the nightingale's beautiful song, the emperor decided to keep the bird with him. He **enclosed** her in a gilded cage, and she sang for the emperor as he ate his supper each night.

One day, the emperor was given the gift of a mechanical nightingale. When it was wound up, it sang beautifully. In contrast to the **commonplace** appearance of the real nightingale, the artificial bird was covered with brightly colored jewels. The emperor was so excited about the new bird that he forgot about the gray nightingale. One day, her cage door was left open, and she flew **stealthily** away to live in the nearby forest. When the emperor finally noticed the bird was gone, he became angry and ordered it to leave his country. The nightingale took up the life of a **nomad, roaming** from forest to forest in neighboring lands. As for the artificial bird, after a while it just stopped working. There was no more music in the palace.

Years later, the emperor became terribly sick. As he lay in bed, the nightingale suddenly appeared and began to sing. Cheered by the beautiful song, the emperor began to feel better, and at last he sat up in bed. "Dear nightingale, I am so sorry I was angry with you," he said **ruefully.** "You have saved my life. Please stay here with me."

"My dear emperor," replied the nightingale, "I prefer to live free in the forest, but I will return to sing to you every night. I will sing to you of all the good and evil in your kingdom. I have only one **plea** to make: Let no one know that a little bird tells you everything!"

WORD LIST

| commonplace |
| enclose |
| magnificent |
| nomad |
| plea |
| roam |
| ruefully |
| stealthily |

1. What is commonplace about the nightingale? What is not?

   The nightingale looks rather plain, but sings beautifully.

2. Use a boldfaced word from the passage in a sentence that describes the nightingale.

   Answers will vary.

C Fit the right word into each sentence. Write the word on the line.

1. "I broke your favorite pen," Rhonda admitted _____ruefully_____ . *(stealthily/ruefully)*

2. Those high stone walls _____enclose_____ a beautiful secret garden. *(enclose/roam)*

3. The burglar crept _____stealthily_____ up the stairs. *(ruefully/stealthily)*

4. The _____magnificent_____ view from the top of the mountain made the climb worthwhile. *(magnificent/commonplace)*

5. I would like to _____roam_____ the world to learn about different cultures. *(roam/enclose)*

D Classify each word from the word list by its part of speech.

Nouns	Verbs	Adverbs	Adjectives
nomad	enclose	stealthily	magnificent
plea	roam	ruefully	commonplace

After students complete the chart, point out that some words, such as the verb *steal,* have a noun form *(stealth),* an adverb form *(stealthily),* and an adjective form *(stealthy).* You may wish to challenge students to see how many forms they can make out of each vocabulary word and add them to the boxes.

OTHER FORMS

enclosed

enclosure

magnificently

plead

pleadingly

roaming

steal

stealth

stealthy

rue

rueful

E Complete each sentence with a phrase that makes sense. Note that some other forms of the vocabulary words have been used.

1. Something you might **enclose** in an envelope is _____

_____ .

2. One **magnificent** view that I have seen is _____

_____ .

3. If you **roam** the world, _____

_____ .

4. You might feel **rueful** about _____

_____ .

5. "Mom," I said **pleadingly**, "may I _____

_____ ?"

ENRICHMENT WORDS

Here are two more words that are examples of different parts of speech.

See page viii for Enrichment Word activities.

1. **din** (dĭn) *A* **din** *is a loud, confused, continuous noise.* (noun)
   The **din** of the construction kept us from concentrating on our lesson.

2. **nimble** (nĭm' bəl) *A* **nimble** *person or animal moves quickly and lightly.*
   (adjective)
   You must be **nimble** to be a good gymnast.

OFF THE PAGE

In Exercise C, you classified parts of speech. Now think of two more words for each part of speech and add them to the correct columns. After you list the words, write one sentence with a word from each column.

nimble

wrench

Double Duty
words that are both nouns and verbs

A Some words do double duty. They can be used as either nouns or verbs. For example, we can walk (a verb) or we can take a walk (a noun). Below are double-duty words that may be nouns or verbs.

1. **feast** (fēst) *A* **feast** *is a large meal (noun). When we feast, we eat a large meal (verb).*
   Dad will cook a huge **feast** to celebrate Thanksgiving (noun). We will **feast** on turkey with all the trimmings (verb).

2. **fool** (fool) *A* **fool** *is a person who does not have good sense and is easy to trick (noun). To* **fool** *someone is to trick her or him (verb).*
   She was a **fool** to believe that the moon was made of cheese (noun). It wasn't nice to **fool** her (verb).

3. **guarantee** (găr' ən tē') *A* **guarantee** *is a promise of quality (noun). When we* **guarantee** *something, we promise that something will work as it should (verb).*
   Our new computer came with a **guarantee** that any problem would be fixed without charge (noun). The company will **guarantee** that we will not be charged for repairs (verb).

4. **marvel** (mär' vəl) *A* **marvel** *is something wonderful that surprises us (noun). When we* **marvel** *at something, we express surprise or wonder (verb).*
   The Internet is a **marvel** of modern technology (noun). I **marvel** at how much we can do with it (verb).

5. **scout** (skout) *A* **scout** *is a person sent to find out information (noun). When we* **scout** *we look for something (verb).*
   A **scout** went ahead to find a stream for the campers (noun). We sent Joe ahead to **scout** for water (verb).

6. **shiver** (shĭv' ər) *A* **shiver** *is a small shaking movement we make because we are cold or afraid (noun). When we* **shiver** *we make small shaking movements (verb).*
   A **shiver** went down my back while watching the scary movie (noun). Walking into an air-conditioned store on a hot day makes me **shiver** (verb).

7. **vow** (vou) *A* **vow** *is a solemn promise. (noun) When we* **vow** *we make a solemn promise. (verb).*
   I made a **vow** to my aunt that I would not get lost in the city (noun). She had me **vow** that I would stay by her side at all times (verb).

8. **wrench** (rĕnch) *A* **wrench** *is a tool for gripping and turning objects (noun). When we* **wrench** *something, we pull or turn it suddenly (verb).*
   I used a **wrench** to turn the rusted faucet (noun). Don't turn the handle too hard, or you might **wrench** it right off the faucet (verb).

Review the definitions of *noun* and *verb*. Then ask whether *feast* is a noun or a verb. Discuss the introduction and the words with students.

All of the boldfaced words in the passage below can be either nouns or verbs. Read the passage. Then answer the questions that follow.

Acapulco—A City of Old and New

Beautiful Acapulco is a Mexican town with a long history. For hundreds of years, native peoples lived there peacefully, but in 1530, the Spanish explorer Hernán Cortez **wrenched** control of the city away from them. The city became a major port for ships that transported spices and silks from Asia to Spain. Soon, English and Dutch pirates began to **scout** out the ships to attack them and steal the valuable cargo. So, in 1617, Fort San Diego was built as a place where ships could land safely. The fort is now used as a museum for the many people who visit each year.

Present-day visitors to Acapulco **marvel** at an unusual bronze statue of a patron saint. The statue was placed underwater in the harbor by fishermen to protect people who work on the water. It can be viewed from a glass-bottomed boat. Divers put flowers at the feet of the statue every year on December 12, the day of the saint.

Another marvel, Acapulco's high-diving *clavadistas*, leap from 120-foot cliffs into the water. Their daring dives send **shivers** down the spines of tourists, but the *clavadistas* are not **fools.** They wait for tides to deepen the water before they dive.

After watching the *clavadistas*, you might want to **feast** on some seafood. Then relax and sit in the sun. Acapulco averages 360 days of sunshine and most of the rain falls at night. Although there is no **guarantee,** it will probably be sunny when you are there. At the end of the day, as you enjoy one of the most beautiful sunsets in the world, you may just **vow** to stay in Acapulco forever.

Name

Date

WORD LIST

WORD LIST

feast
fool
guarantee
marvel
scout
shiver
vow
wrench

1. Which sights of Acapulco would make you marvel most?

   Students should support their answer with details from the passage.

2. List two words used as nouns and two words used as verbs from the passage.

   Nouns: feast, shivers, fools, guarantee

   Verbs: wrenched, scout, marvel, vow

C Choose the word that best fits in each sentence. Write the word on the line. Then write the part of speech.

1. The basketball player was nervous because he knew a *(scout/fool)* was at the game. _____ scout

   Part of speech: _____ noun

2. I wish my talkative little sister would take a *(fool/vow)* of silence. _____ vow   Part of speech: _____ noun

3. I *(guarantee/feast)* that you will enjoy that video game. _____ guarantee   Part of speech: _____ verb

4. The frightening tale sent a *(vow/shiver)* of fear up my spine. _____ shiver   Part of speech: _____ noun

5. You will *(fool/marvel)* at the dinosaur exhibit in the museum. _____ marvel   Part of speech: _____ verb

D Add the word from the word list that is a **synonym** for the words in each list.

After students complete the exercise, ask them to identify whether each response is a noun or a verb.

1. look for, search for, find out, explore, _____ scout

2. amazing thing, spectacle, wonderful thing, astonishing thing, _____ marvel

3. trick, deceive, mislead, _____ fool

4. festival, big meal, banquet, celebration, _____ feast

5. tremble, quiver, shake, shudder, _____ shiver

© Great Source DO NOT COPY

© Great Source DO NOT COPY

Lesson 8 **31**

E Complete each sentence with a phrase that makes sense. Note that some other forms of the vocabulary words are used in the sentences.

1. A **foolish** idea can _____

_____ .

2. An example of a **marvelous** event is _____

_____ .

3. I would like to **guarantee** that _____

_____ .

4. You can use a **wrench** to _____

_____ .

5. For a special **feast,** I would serve _____

_____ .

ENRICHMENT WORDS

Here are two more words that can be both a noun and a verb.

1. maneuver (mə noo' ver) *To* **maneuver** *is to put a clever plan into action* (verb). *A* **maneuver** *is a skilled or clever step toward a goal* (noun).

   Leo will **maneuver** his bike into the inside track (verb).
   This **maneuver** will help him win the race (noun).

2. rebuke (rĭ byook') *To* **rebuke** *is to blame or criticize in a sharp way* (verb). *A* **rebuke** *is a sharp criticism* (noun).

   Our teacher threatened to **rebuke** us for talking too much (verb).
   After our teacher's **rebuke,** we were quiet (noun).

See page viii for Enrichment Word activities.

OFF THE PAGE

Many things come with **guarantees.** For example, many computer companies guarantee that the programs they sell will work for a year, or they will replace them for free. Look at home and at school to locate something that comes with a guarantee. Describe the guarantee. Do you think it is a good one?

Same but Different
words with multiple meanings

A Many English words have more than one meaning. One dictionary lists more than 30 meanings for the common word *run!* All of the words below have at least two meanings.

1. **arm** (ärm) *An **arm** is an upper limb of the body connecting the hand and wrist to the shoulder* (noun). *To **arm** means to carry or supply with weapons or something that strengthens* (verb).
I carried three towels on my left **arm.** When you go to the beach, **arm** yourself with lots of sunscreen.

2. **charge** (chärj) *A **charge** is a price* (noun). *To **charge** may mean to ask a price or to rush forward* (verb).
The **charge** for the movie was five dollars. Theaters **charge** five dollars for the movie.

3. **dash** (dăsh) *To **dash** means to run quickly; it also means to destroy, especially hopes* (verb).
The racers will **dash** to the finish line. Nothing can **dash** our hopes of winning the championship.

4. **depression** (dĭ prĕsh' ən) *A **depression** is a low spot or hollow surrounded by higher places. It is also the state of feeling sad* (noun).
The boy's handprint made a **depression** in the newly poured concrete. After her brother became ill, Amyra went into a **depression.**

5. **gorge** (gôrj) *A **gorge** is a narrow valley surrounded by steep walls* (noun). *To **gorge** is to stuff oneself with food* (verb).
The hiker slid down the steep, rocky sides of the **gorge.** If you **gorge** yourself with food, you may get sick.

6. **roll** (rōl) *To **roll** is to turn over and over* (verb). *A **roll** is a continuous series of short beats on a drum* (noun).
We watched the ball **roll** along the sidewalk. The singer was introduced with a dramatic minute-long drum **roll.**

7. **skirt** (skûrt) *A **skirt** is a piece of clothing that hangs from the waist* (noun). *To **skirt** is to move around the edge of something* (verb).
Tanya prefers to wear pants instead of a **skirt.** We can avoid the traffic if we **skirt** the city.

8. **yarn** (yärn) *Yarn is a thick strand of twisted thread used in knitting and weaving. A **yarn** is also a long and exaggerated story* (noun).
My mother knit the **yarn** into a warm sweater. Grandfather would often amuse us with a **yarn** about his sailing days.

Ask students what *charge* means. Point out that some words have very different meanings and that students need to rely on the context to know which definition is correct. Connect the words to Lesson 8, which was about words that can be either a noun or a verb.

All the boldfaced words in the passage below have more than one meaning. You can determine the correct meaning by using context. Read the passage. Then answer the questions.

A Paradise in Asia

Explorers in Asia often heard **yarns** of a hidden paradise with a beautiful waterfall located deep within Tibet. Author James Hilton wrote a novel about this paradise, calling it "Shangri-la." Did it really exist? In 1911 and 1924, explorers tried to find Shangri-la and failed. In 1998 the hopes of more explorers were **dashed** when the search was called off because of the accidental death of a team member.

Finally, in 1999, a team headed by National Geographic explorers made a discovery—the Hidden Falls of the Tsangpo. The explorers prepared carefully and went slowly. Past accidents have shown that people cannot **charge** carelessly into wild country and dangerous mountain ranges.

In the Himalayan wilderness, a deep **gorge** leads to another deep gorge. A waterfall in the inner part drops 100 feet into a **depression.** Two men, Ian Baker and Ken Storm, Jr., entered the inner gorge while their companions **skirted** the edge of the first gorge. They **rolled** out traditional mountain-climbing rope to help them go down the last 80 feet to the waterfall. But they were also **armed** with more modern equipment, such as laser range-finders, which they used to measure the depth of the gorge and the height of the waterfall.

Although they had to **dash** back home to report their discovery, the explorers, like the people in James Hilton's story, did not want to leave their Shangri-la.

1. What is the meaning of **gorge** in the passage? How do you know?

   Gorge means "steep valley" because it is in the wilderness and it is deep.

2. What is the meaning of **depression** in the passage? How do you know?

   Depression means "low spot" because a waterfall drops into it.

WORD LIST

arm

charge

dash

depression

gorge

roll

skirt

yarn

C Write the word from the word list that can be used as a **synonym** for each underlined word or phrase.

1. I'm just going to <u>run quickly</u> to the corner store to buy some milk.
   _____dash_____

2. After eating take-out food for two weeks, I wanted to <u>stuff</u> myself on Mom's cooking. _____gorge_____

3. "We don't <u>ask a price</u> for a refill on soda," said the waiter.
   _____charge_____

4. Building a bridge across a <u>deep valley</u> takes great engineering skill.
   _____gorge_____

5. The stray moose had to be calmed down when he began to <u>rush forward</u> toward the crowd. _____charge_____

D Complete the crossword puzzle, using words from the word box.

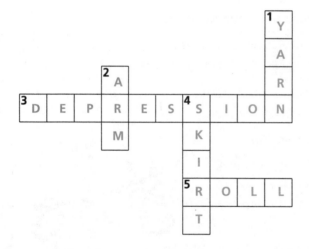

Challenge students to make their own crosword puzzles to use more of the words.

Across

3. sadness; hollow
5. turn over and over; drum beat

Down

1. tale; thread
2. supply with weapons; limb
4. walk around something; clothing

OTHER FORMS

dashed
disarm
engorge
unarmed
unroll

E Complete each sentence with a phrase that makes sense. Some other forms of the vocabulary words are used.

1. A **gorge** looks like _____

   _____ .

2. When your hopes are **dashed,** _____

   _____ .

3. People who are **unarmed** do not have _____

   _____ .

4. Something made out of **yarn** is _____

   _____ .

5. An example of something that you can **unroll** is _____

   _____ .

Discuss how the prefix *un-* changes the meaning of *armed.*

ENRICHMENT WORDS

Here are two more words that have more than one meaning.

1. **counter** (koun' tər) *When you* **counter** *something, you act against it* (verb). *A* **counter** *is a long table or cabinet top* (noun).

   An aspirin may **counter** the pain from a mild injury. People often cut vegetables on a kitchen **counter.**

2. **medium** (mē' dē əm) **Medium** *is a point in the middle, between two extremes, such as small and large* (adjective). *A* **medium** *(plural* **media***) is a material or technique used for producing art or communication* (noun).

   We bought **medium** size eggs, rather than large ones. Watercolor is a popular **medium** for children's art.

See page viii for Enrichment Word activities.

OFF THE PAGE

Charge, dash, and **roll** have even more meanings than are listed in this lesson. Use a dictionary to find out one other meaning for each word. Write sentences or draw pictures that explain the words so that you can tell someone another meaning and the part of speech.

Review
Lessons 6-9

In this lesson, you will review the words and strategies you have learned in the last four lessons. This will help you to remember them when you read and write.

A **MATCHING WORDS AND DEFINITIONS**
Write the word from the box that matches each definition.

| plea | marvel | vow | magnificent | enclose | arm |

1. excellent or wonderful _____magnificent_____

2. an urgent request or call for help _____plea_____

3. a solemn promise _____vow_____

4. to carry or supply with weapons _____arm_____

5. something wonderful and surprising _____marvel_____

6. put inside something _____enclose_____

B **USING WORDS IN CONTEXT** Use the words in each box to complete the paragraphs.

| guarantee | vowed | stealthily | fool | yarns |

The politician was a skilled campaigner. He had a way of making everyone happy. He told amusing **(1)** _____yarns_____ about his childhood and made people laugh. Then he told sad stories of poor people, and the crowd listened with solemn faces. But he **(2)** _____stealthily_____ avoided making any promises. He would not **(3)** _____guarantee_____ anything to us. When I heard him, I **(4)** _____vowed_____ to myself that I would never be like him. I would not try to **(5)** _____fool_____ people into voting for me. I would be an honest and straightforward politician.

| shiver | commonplace | gorge | dash | feast |

The sights when you swim underwater can be a

(6) _____feast_____ for the eyes. It is (7) _____commonplace_____

to see exquisite coral formations. Schools of brightly colored fish

(8) _____dash_____ quickly from place to place. A friend of mine

once found herself so close to an octopus it made her (9) _____shiver_____

with excitement! She half expected the strange creature to start speaking to

her, as if she were in a science-fiction movie. Instead, it seemed to ignore

her and disappeared into a deep (10) _____gorge_____ far below.

C **PARTS OF SPEECH** Write *noun* or *verb* to tell the part of speech of the boldfaced word in each sentence.

1. It has been about 65 million years since dinosaurs **roamed** the earth.
   _____verb_____

2. The new car came with a **guarantee** for parts and labor.
   _____noun_____

3. Stacey was so upset about losing the gardening competition, she began
   to **wrench** the plants from the ground. _____verb_____

4. The farmer decided to **enclose** the pasture with a fence.
   _____verb_____

5. Because of the rocky ground, we had to **scout** for a flat place to pitch
   our tents. _____verb_____

6. Bedouins are **nomads** who live in the deserts of the Middle East and
   Northern Africa. _____noun_____

MULTIPLE-MEANING WORDS Circle the correct part of speech and definition for the boldfaced word.

1. I couldn't believe he had the nerve to **charge** five dollars for a hot dog!

   (*verb:* ask a price)   *noun:* the price of something

2. The ancient site had been such a popular spot for grinding grain that a **depression** had formed in the rock.

   (*noun:* low spot or hollow)   *noun:* the state of feeling sad

3. The stunned crowd stood silently watching the truckload of pipes **roll** down Main Street.

   noun: continuous series of short beats on a drum

   (*verb:* turn over and over)

4. According to family legend, the blanket was knitted from the finest **yarn** available.

   (*noun:* thick strand of thread)   *noun:* exaggerated story

5. While the hikers ate their lunch by the edge of the **gorge,** they were treated to a breathtaking view.

   (*noun:* steep, rocky valley)   *verb:* stuff oneself with food

6. When she lost the race, Sylvia's hopes of ever getting to the district finals were **dashed.**

   verb: ran quickly   (*verb:* destroyed)

7. To keep our feet dry, we tried to **skirt** the edge of the puddle.

   verb: (step around)   *noun:* clothing

8. Mom and Dad keep a **wrench** in the toolkit in the car, just in case.

   verb: pull suddenly   (*noun:* a tool)

TEST-TAKING STRATEGIES (Analogies) Remember that an **analogy** compares word pairs that are related in some way. Analogies also appear on many tests, so practicing them will make you a better test taker.

If students have little or no experience with analogies, model how to solve an analogy by thinking out loud. See also Lesson 5.

Strategy: The key to solving analogies is figuring out how the words are related. Three kinds of relationships are shown in the analogies below.

1. **kind, or type, of** (*soccer* is a kind of *sport*)
2. **synonym** (*scared* is a synonym for *frightened*)
3. **antonym** (*ill* is an antonym of *healthy*)

Directions: Choose the word that completes each analogy and write it on the line.

1. Ruefully is to regretfully as happily is to _____gladly_____ .
   gladly/sadly

2. Intelligent is to smart as commonplace is to _____ordinary_____ .
   foolish/ordinary

3. Hamlet is to village as meal is to _____feast_____ . *feast/eat*

4. Closed is to open as terrible is to _____magnificent_____ .
   magnificent/emaciated

5. Green is to color as gorge is to _____valley_____ . *valley/plaza*

See page 127 for a reproducible test in standardized-test format.

ENRICHMENT WORDS

Draw a line between each Enrichment Word and its definition.

1. nimble — point in the middle/material for producing art
2. din — act against/long table top
3. rebuke — blame or criticize/sharp criticism
4. maneuver — moving quickly and lightly
5. counter — loud continuous noise
6. medium — clever step toward a goal/steer around

THINKING WITH WORDS
Skill Lesson
using context

When you come across an unfamiliar word in your reading, you can often figure out its meaning by using the **context.** A word's context is the group of words and sentences around it.

 SENTENCE CONTEXT When you use context clues, you combine your reading, your knowledge of how words and sentences work, and your general knowledge to figure out the meaning of an unknown word. Suppose you are reading about the human body and come across this sentence:

> Hairs grow from **follicles** in the **dermis,** the inner, deeper layer of the skin.

You can use common sense to figure out a lot about the words that may be unfamiliar, *follicles* and *dermis.* In fact, the word *dermis* is defined in the sentence.

1. Write the words that you can use to figure out what *dermis* means. Then write a meaning for the word.   <u>the inner, deeper layer of the skin;</u>

   <u>*dermis* means the inner, deeper layer of the skin</u>

2. Now you can use the meaning of the word *dermis* to help you with *follicle.* Think about what *dermis* means and what you already know about hair from your own experience. What do you think follicles are?

   <u>little holes or places in the skin where hair grows</u>

This was all done by thinking with words, or using context. You did not have to interrupt your reading to look up the new words in the dictionary. If you wish, you can take the time to add to your understanding of the new words by using a dictionary at the end of your reading.

B **SUBSTITUTION CONTEXT CLUES** Rereading the example sentence on page 41 and substituting the phrase *tiny holes* for *follicles* helped you make sense of the sentence. When you did this, you were using **substitution context clues.** This is when you substitute another word or phrase for the unknown word to help you make sense of text. Here is another example in which the substitution method of context clues can help you figure out unfamiliar words.

Review students' answers together so that everyone understands how to use context to figure out the meaning of an unknown word.

As a volcano erupts, the hot, **molten** rock flows down the mountainside.

Since the rock is hot and flows, the word *melted* would be a good substitute for *molten*: As the volcano erupts, the hot, **melted** rock flows down the mountainside.

Now you try. Choose the best substitute for the boldfaced word in the sentences. Circle your answer.

1. The store owner appeared to be **prosperous,** with her diamond necklace and designer clothing.   tasteful   (successful)

2. News traveled from city to city throughout the **realm** that the golden knight had defeated the enemy.   house   (kingdom)

3. "Alas," said the dying hero. "I am a mere **mortal** and cannot live forever."   (human)   injury

4. Because she had delayed calling the doctor, the pain had worsened and become quite **acute.**   (sharp)   recent

5. The exhausted dog was so sound asleep that he was not even **responsive** to the loud noise of the crowd.   (reacting)   dreaming

realm

DEFINING CONTEXT CLUES If you look back at the example sentence on page 41, you will see that you used another kind of context clue to help you figure out the meaning of the word *dermis*. In that case, the word was defined for you right in the sentence. This is called a **defining context clue.**

One clue to readers that a definition follows the word is the use of commas, as in the example with *dermis*. The defining clue is the phrase "the inner, deeper layer of the skin," which follows the comma after *dermis*. Other signs of a defining context clue are the use of parentheses, dashes, or words such as *or*.

> The teenager tried to **emulate** *(or imitate)* the movie star's appearance.
>
> The teenager tried to **emulate**—*or imitate*—the movie star's appearance.
>
> The teenager tried to **emulate**, *or imitate*, the movie star's appearance.

Now try these examples. Underline the words in the sentence that tell you the meaning of the boldfaced word. Then write the word's definition.

1. Sharks have a reputation of being fierce **predators,** <u>animals that hunt and feed on other animals</u>.

   A predator is ___<u>an animal that hunts and feeds on other animals</u>___ .

2. The world's largest **crustacean** (<u>shellfish</u>) is the giant spider crab, which has a leg span of almost 13 feet.

   A crustacean is ___<u>a shellfish</u>___ .

3. In the Middle Ages, knights would have tournaments in which one would try to **dislodge** another knight from his horse with a **lance;** that is to say, <u>the knights tried to knock each other off their horses using long spears</u>.

   To dislodge is ___<u>to knock someone off of something</u>___ .

   A lance is ___<u>a long spear</u>___ .

OPPOSITE CONTEXT CLUES There is another kind of context clue to help you figure out the meaning of an unfamiliar word. Sometimes writers help you know what something means by telling you what it does <u>not</u> mean. This is called an **opposite context clue.** Be on the lookout for words such as *not, no, rather, but*, and *however* to help you find opposite context clues. Here are some examples:

> Our business was <u>not</u> **inundated** with calls on our first day, <u>but</u> we did receive one or two requests. (Since one or two calls is <u>not</u> being inundated, you can figure out that *inundated* must mean getting a lot of something.)
>
> I would <u>rather</u> be **jubilant** than depressed. (The word *rather* lets you know that *jubilant* means *happy*, the opposite of *depressed*.)
>
> Roberto thought the fund raiser would be quite **lucrative,** <u>but</u> the other team members thought it wouldn't raise any money. (The word *but* tells you that Roberto's opinion was the opposite of the rest of the team's. *Lucrative* must mean raising a lot of money.)

Write the letter of the word or phrase that means about the same as the boldfaced word.

1. At first the opposing team seemed **invincible,** but in the end, they were easily beaten. ____a____
   a. unbeatable   **b.** snobby   **c.** unpredictable

2. The animal was not a **vertebrate** because it had no backbone. ____c____
   a. an animal with ears
   b. an animal with four legs
   c. an animal with a spine

3. Senator Goldstein had not been elected to the Senate; rather he had been **appointed** by the governor when the former senator died. ____b____
   a. elected by a majority of voters
   b. assigned or chosen by someone else
   c. elected by a committee

4. The **rebellion** was not a success. At the end of the fighting, conditions remained as they had been. ____a____
   a. violent uprising   **b.** quiet complaint   **c.** calm cooperation

vertebrates

Words for a New Nation
words from social studies

 A This lesson presents words you will often find when you study history or read historical fiction. Many relate to the time of the American Revolutionary war, but you will also find them in books dealing with other eras or about government.

1. **abolish** (ə bŏl' ĭsh) *To* **abolish** *is to end rules, laws, or something in government.* (verb)
Colonists wanted the king to **abolish** the tax on tea.

2. **appointed** (ə poin' tĭd) *A person who is* **appointed** *to a job is chosen or assigned by someone else.* (adjective)
Sent by the King of England, **appointed** governors served the American colonies.

3. **apprentice** (ə prĕn' tĭs) *An* **apprentice** *is a person who learns to do a job by working with someone skilled in the job.* (noun)
In colonial times, a young boy served as an **apprentice** in candle making, carpentry, or printing.

4. **carriage** (kăr' ĭj) *A* **carriage** *is a wagon, usually pulled by horses, used to carry people.* (noun)
The **carriage** carried passengers from Houston to Austin in three days.

5. **elected** (ĭ lĕk' tĭd) *A person who is* **elected** *is chosen by vote for a job or office.* (adjective)
Elected members of the U.S. Congress are chosen by their districts.

6. **prosperous** (prŏs' pər əs) *A* **prosperous** *person has wealth, or money, and is successful.* (adjective)
The store owner started out poor but became **prosperous**.

7. **rebellion** (rĭ bĕl' yən) *A* **rebellion**, *or uprising, takes place when people fight against their own government.* (noun)
American colonists threw chests of tea into Boston Harbor as a **rebellion** against high taxes.

8. **representative** (rĕp' rĭ zĕn' tə tĭv) *A* **representative** *is a person elected or chosen to act for a group of people.* (noun)
Our class chose a **representative** to serve on the school council.

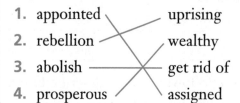

Draw a line between each vocabulary word and its definition.

1. appointed   uprising
2. rebellion   wealthy
3. abolish ——————   get rid of
4. prosperous   assigned

Review that the U.S. government is made up of elected officials who represent the people, but that prior to the Revolutionary War, the colonies were under the rule of England.

The boldfaced words in the passage below are connected to the time of the American Revolution. Read the passage. Then answer the questions that follow.

Benjamin Franklin: A Man of Many Talents

"He snatched the lightning from the skies," said someone about Benjamin Franklin. Born in 1706, Franklin was the 15th of 17 children. At age ten, he began to work for his brother as a printer's **apprentice.**

When he was 17, Franklin decided to start a new life in Philadelphia. There he published *Poor Richard's Almanac,* a collection of practical wisdom that made him **prosperous.** Franklin was **appointed** Deputy Postmaster of Philadelphia. He also invented the lightning rod.

After he was **elected** to the Pennsylvania Assembly, Franklin was sent to England as a **representative** of the American colonies. In 1775, he returned to Philadelphia to find that open **rebellion** against Britain had begun. Franklin became caught up in the American Revolution. He went to Canada in an attempt to get support for the Revolution. The trip was a failure, but on his return, Franklin was asked to take part in writing the Declaration of Independence. Then he traveled to France to get support for the revolutionary army.

When he returned in 1785, the war had been won and British rule had been **abolished.** But the colonies needed a government of their own. Franklin, then 81, was asked to attend the Constitutional Convention that would establish this government. Too weak to travel by **carriage,** he was carried to and from the convention in a special chair.

1. What is one of Franklin's most important accomplishments? Tell why you think so.

   Students might suggest *Poor Richard's Almanac,* his participation in writing the

   Declaration of Independence, or his contributions to the Constitutional Convention.

2. All of the following words describe Franklin in some way. Choose two of the words and explain your choices.

   apprentice   elected   rebellion   representative

   Answers should show that the student understands the words.

WORD LIST

| abolish |
| appointed |
| apprentice |
| carriage |
| elected |
| prosperous |
| rebellion |
| representative |

C Choose the word from the two choices given that best fits in each sentence. Write the word on the line.

1. One job of the president is to fill (*abolished/appointed*) positions. _____appointed_____

2. The newly (*elected/abolished*) president of the student council won by a huge majority of students. _____elected_____

3. Some American colonists did not want to join in the (*carriage/rebellion*) against British rule. _____rebellion_____

4. Our school sent a (*rebellion/representative*) to speak to the school board about a new gym. _____representative_____

5. By going to business school, Tim hoped to become a (*prosperous/apprentice*) business owner. _____prosperous_____

D In Lesson 11, you learned about using context to figure out new words. Below are some sentences that contain unfamiliar words. These words are boldfaced. Read each sentence. Underline the words that help you figure out the meaning of the new word. Then circle the word that is a synonym. Think of definition, substitution, and opposite context clues as you do this exercise.

1. The **flourishing** businesswoman bought a huge boat.

   (*prosperous*)   *elected*

2. The **conveyance**, or wagon, was on display in the museum.

   (*carriage*)   *rebellion*

3. The people did not elect the superintendent of education; it was an **assigned** job.   (*appointed*)   *prosperous*

4. The school board did not continue the job of assistant principal, but rather they **terminated** it.   *rebellion*   (*abolished*)

5. The **novice**, a learner, was just out of school.

   (*apprentice*)   *prosperous*

As you review each sentence with students, have them explain how they figured out the meaning of the bold-faced word.

OTHER FORMS

appointment

apprenticeship

election

prosperity

rebel

rebellious

represent

E Complete each sentence with a phrase that makes sense. Note that some other forms of the vocabulary words are used in the sentences.

1. A **rebellious** attitude can lead to _____

_____ .

2. I would like to **abolish** _____

_____ .

3. A sign of **prosperity** is _____

_____ .

4. An **apprenticeship** would be helpful to learn about _____

_____ .

5. A **carriage** is used to _____

_____ .

ENRICHMENT WORDS

Here are two more words that will help you read about government, history, and historical fiction.

1. **convene** (kən vēn') *To* **convene** *is to assemble together for an official purpose.*

   Leaders of the new American nation **convened** the Continental Congress to discuss forming a government.

2. **proclamation** (prok' lə mā' shən) *A* **proclamation** *is a public announcement or statement.* (noun)

   The Declaration of Independence was a **proclamation** of freedom from British rule.

proclamation

See page viii for Enrichment Word activities.

OFF THE PAGE

In most states the governor appoints a state superintendent of education to set school policy. Do you feel that this should be an **elected** or an **appointed** position? Explain your answer.

LESSON 13

Making Sense
words from science

a vertebrate

A Science teaches us much about the animal world. The words in this lesson will help you to describe animals and the senses that they use to see, hear, smell, taste, and feel their world.

1. **acute** (ə kyo͞ot') *Something* **acute** *is very sensitive and sharp.* (adjective)
The eagle's **acute** vision allows it to see small animals from miles away.

2. **auditory** (ŏ' dĭ tôr' ē) **Auditory** *refers to the sense of hearing.* (adjective)
Listening to music is an **auditory** experience.

3. **olfactory** (ŏl făk' tə rē) **Olfactory** *refers to the sense of smell.* (adjective)
Even though snakes don't see or hear very well, they have an excellent **olfactory** sense.

4. **predator** (prĕd' ə tər) *A* **predator** *is an animal that hunts and feeds on other animals.* (noun)
Sharks are **predators** that feed on smaller fish.

5. **responsive** (rĭ spŏn' sĭv) *Something that is* **responsive** *reacts to something else.* (adjective)
A cat's eyes are **responsive** to light; the pupils become smaller in bright light.

6. **species** (spē' shēz) *A* **species** *is a group of similar animals or plants that can produce young.* (noun)
All breeds of dogs belong to the same **species.**

7. **tactile** (tăk' təl) **Tactile** *refers to the sense of touch.* (adjective)
The antenna is the **tactile** organ an ant uses to feel its world.

8. **vertebrate** (vûr' tə brĭt) *A* **vertebrate** *is an animal with a backbone.* (noun)
Vertebrates include fish, amphibians, reptiles, birds, and mammals.

Draw a line between each vocabulary word and its definition.

1. species — sense of hearing
2. auditory — sharp
3. tactile — sense of touch
4. acute — group of similar animals
5. responsive — an animal with a backbone
6. vertebrate — reactive
7. olfactory — sense of hearing
8. auditory — sense of smell

Reproduce the T-chart on page xiii for each student. Have students categorize the words they recognize and the words they find unfamiliar. Have students share what they know about the words before formally introducing them.

All the boldfaced words in the passage below relate to science. Read the passage. Then answer the questions that follow.

The Five Senses of Whales

How does a whale see, hear, taste, feel, and smell? Like human beings, whales are **vertebrates** and mammals. But, of course, a whale's senses must be specially adapted to life in water.

A whale's eyes are placed on the sides of its head, so each eye sees different things. Because deep water is dark, the whale's eyes let in as much light as possible. Some whales can widen their eyes, showing the white part, to express anger. Whales have small **olfactory** organs; their blowholes are used only for breathing, not smelling. Like our **species,** whales have taste buds on their tongues.

Whales have a **tactile** sense and they like to be rubbed gently. Although they are **predators** of other animals, whales show affection to each other. A baby whale is **responsive** to the comforting feel of a mother's body.

The whale's most **acute** sense is its hearing. Whales communicate using low moans, squeals, grunts, whistles, and cries. The sounds of the blue whale can travel sixty miles!

Whales also listen to their own voices to get information. In "echolocation," whales make sounds so high that humans cannot hear them. These sounds bounce, or echo, off objects in the ocean. The sounds enable whales to locate food and swim without bumping into caves and reefs. A whale seems to gather as much information from its **auditory** sense as a human being gathers from vision.

Amazingly, whales are always using their senses. Only one half of a whale's brain sleeps at a time, while the other half is sensing the outside world.

WORD LIST

acute

auditory

olfactory

predator

responsive

species

tactile

vertebrate

1. What is the most surprising thing you learned about whales? Explain.

   Students' answers should reflect an understanding of the passage.

2. Explain how each of the following terms relates to the senses.

   olfactory Olfactory describes the sense of smell.

   tactile Tactile describes the sense of touch.

   auditory Auditory describes the sense of hearing.

C Choose the word from the two choices given that best fits in each sentence. Write the word on the line.

1. A well-trained horse is *(responsive/auditory)* to its trainer's commands.
   responsive

2. In science we are going to study animals that have backbones, or *(predators/vertebrates)*. vertebrates

3. My dad grows only local *(species/vertebrates)* of plants in his garden.
   species

4. Coyotes are *(predators/species)* that hunt and feed on smaller animals, such as rodents. predators

5. The bobcat's *(tactile/acute)* hearing picked up the soft rustle of a mouse in the underbrush. acute

D Think about the words **olfactory, tactile,** and **auditory.** Then write each word above the column where it fits best. Finally, add three words that fit to the bottom part of each box.

Auditory	Olfactory	Tactile
noise	scent	rough
sounds	smell	touch
screech	odor	slimy
possible additions:	possible additions:	possible additions:
howl	perfume	feel
hearing	fragrance	smooth
creak	stink	sting

Name

Date

OTHER FORMS
acuity
auditorium
invertebrate
predatory
response
unresponsive

E Complete each sentence with a phrase that makes sense. Some other forms of the vocabulary words are used.

1. An example of a **predator** is _____ .

2. An example of an **invertebrate** is _____ .

3. A dangerous **species** on earth is _____ .

4. If you lose your **olfactory** sense, _____
_____ .

5. You could go to an **auditorium** to _____
___ _____ .

ENRICHMENT WORDS

Here are two more words that you might use in science.

See page viii for Enrichment Word activities.

1. **dormant** (dôr' mənt) *A plant or animal that is* **dormant** *is not active for a period of time.* (adjective)

   Many plants go into a **dormant** state when they do not have enough water.

2. **nutritious** (noo trĭsh' əs) *A food that is* **nutritious** *gives us the nutrients, or substances, needed for life, growth, and health.*

   Carrots and broccoli are **nutritious** because they contain lots of vitamins.

OFF THE PAGE

Your senses alert you to both pleasant and unpleasant things. For example, a rose has a pleasant smell, or olfactory sensation. However, a skunk gives off an unpleasant smell. Pick one of the senses (olfactory, auditory, tactile) and list three pleasant and three unpleasant sensations.

© Great Source DO NOT COPY

52 Thinking with Words

LESSON 14
Traditional Tales
words from myths

A Ancient peoples needed to explain the forces of nature that they could not understand. Why did the sun rise and set? Why did the seasons change? To do this, they invented traditional tales called "myths." The words in this lesson relate to myths.

Use a word web (see page xii) to collect information about the word myth.

1. **myth** (mĭth) *A* **myth** *is a traditional legend or story about ancestors, heroes, or gods.* (noun)
   In one Greek **myth,** Icarus tried to fly, but the sun melted his wax wings.

2. **fate** (fāt) **Fate** *is an outcome that has been decided upon ahead of time.* (noun)
   In Greek myth, the **fate** of Sisyphus was to forever roll a stone up a hill, only to have it tumble down again.

3. **immortal** (ĭ môr' tl) *Someone who is* **immortal** *lives forever.* (adjective)
   According to Greek myth, gods like Zeus, Athena, and Apollo were **immortal.**

4. **invincible** (ĭn vĭn' sə bəl) *Someone who is* **invincible** *cannot be defeated.* (adjective)
   According to Greek myth, the warrior Achilles was **invincible,** except in one weak spot—his heel.

5. **mortal** (môr' tl) *Someone who is* **mortal** *is human and cannot live forever.* (adjective)
   In Greek mythology, a **mortal** being, Psyche, loved an immortal god, Eros.

6. **psyche** (sī' kē) *A* **psyche** *is a person's state of mind or spirit.* (noun)
   Matthew didn't let his defeat in the swimming finals affect his **psyche.**

7. **realm** (rĕlm) *A* **realm** *is the land, or kingdom, that a king or queen rules.* (noun)
   In Greek myth, the underworld was the **realm** of the god Hades.

8. **timeless** (tīm' lĭs) *Something* **timeless** *is not affected by time and seems to last forever.* (adjective)
   Myths have a **timeless** quality because people behaved much the same then as now.

Draw a line between each vocabulary word and its definition.

1. mortal — state of mind
2. psyche — outcome decided already
3. myth — human
4. fate — traditional story
5. immortal — unbeatable
6. invincible — living forever

All the boldfaced words in the passage below are related to myths. Read the passage. Then answer the questions that follow.

Persephone and Demeter

Like most cultures, the Ancient Greeks had a tradition of **myths,** or stories, that explained the forces of nature. The myths centered on gods who had all the faults of **mortal** human beings. People have been repeating these myths for more than 2,500 years, which proves their **timeless** appeal.

The myth of how winter came to be shows how the **immortal** gods, acting out of revenge and jealousy, influenced the **fate** of humans. Long ago, the earth was a green paradise warmed all year by Demeter, the goddess of agriculture. Demeter had a beautiful daughter named Persephone. One day, Persephone wandered away to explore a field of flowers. Unfortunately, Hades, god of the underworld, happened to be visiting the earth. When he saw Persephone, he fell in love with her and carried her off

to his underworld **realm** to be his bride.

Demeter was desperate to get her daughter back. Her **psyche** was so affected that she forgot to warm the world. Soon it fell into endless winter. Finally, she spoke to Zeus, king of the gods. Zeus was **invincible,** and all of the gods would follow his orders. Demeter complained to Zeus, and he agreed to let Persephone return home, but only if she had not eaten anything.

Unfortunately, Persephone had eaten six seeds. So Demeter and Hades struck a deal. Persephone would stay with her mother for six months and with Hades for six months. When Persephone is with her mother, Demeter happily warms the earth, and we have summer. When Persephone is with Hades, Demeter is sad and we have winter.

1. Choose two of the following vocabulary words. Write a sentence for each word that explains how it relates to Demeter.

   fate   myth   immortal   realm

   Students' answers should show that they understand the vocabulary words.

2. How can you tell from the context what *myth* means?

   Myth is used as a synonym for story, and the text says that myths explained

   the forces of nature.

myth

fate

immortal

invincible

mortal

psyche

realm

timeless

C Choose the word from the two choices given that best fits in each sentence. Write the word on the line.

1. The ancient _____myth_____ (realm/myth) explained the origin of the sun.

2. The book *Tuck Everlasting* deals with _____immortals_____ (immortals/mortals) who do not grow old and die.

3. The beauty of the ancient Greek statue is _____timeless_____ (invincible/timeless), and it is still lovely even after 4000 years.

4. My _____psyche_____ (realm/psyche) was helped by the many compliments I received.

5. Sometimes things just seem to happen because of _____fate_____ (psyche/fate) and are beyond our control.

D In Lesson 11, you learned about using context to figure out new words. Below are some sentences that contain unfamiliar words. These words are boldfaced. Read each sentence. Underline the words that help you figure out the meaning of the new word. Then circle the word that is a synonym. Think of definition, substitution, and opposite context clues as you do this exercise.

1. The **impregnable** fort <u>did not fall to the enemy</u>.
   (invincible)   immortal

2. Human beings <u>cannot always decide their own</u> **karma.**
   (fate)   timeless

3. The **domain** of the Spanish <u>king</u> once <u>included much of South America.</u>   (realm)   mortal

4. The **fabrications** <u>told by the ancient Norse people explained the creation of the world.</u>   mortals   (myths)

5. The story of Cinderella seems **eternal** because it has been <u>told in different versions for thousands of years.</u>   (timeless)   invincible

As you review each sentence with students, have them explain how they figured out the meaning of the bold-faced word.

OTHER FORMS

mythology

fateful

immortality

mortality

timelessness

E Complete each sentence with a phrase that makes sense. Note that some other forms of the vocabulary words are used in the sentences.

1. A character in Greek **mythology** is _____ .

2. If I were **immortal,** _____ .

3. Zeus wanted everyone in his **realm** to _____ .

4. I wonder if it is my **fate** to _____

_____ .

5. Something that affects my **psyche** is _____

_____ .

See page viii for
Enrichment Word
activities.

ENRICHMENT WORDS

Here are two more words that you can use to talk about mythology.

1. **deity** (dē' ĭ tē) *A* **deity** *is a god or goddess.* (noun)

   According to Greek myth, Neptune was the **deity** who ruled the sea.

2. **Olympian** (ō lĭm' pē ən) **Olympian** *refers to Mount Olympus, where the Greek gods were said to have lived. It can also mean anything that is very powerful or godlike. This word is related to the Olympic games, which were started by the Ancient Greeks to honor their gods.* (adjective)

   The Greek god Zeus had **Olympian** powers because he ruled heaven and earth.

OFF THE PAGE

The stories about superheroes that appear in comics, television, and movies might be called modern **myths.** Describe your favorite superheroes. In what way do stories about them seem like myths?

LESSON 15

Review
lessons 11–14

In this lesson, you will review the words and skills you have learned in the last four lessons. This will help you to remember them.

A **MATCHING WORDS AND DEFINITIONS**
Write the word from the box that matches each definition.

> invincible   fate   appointed   species   elected   immortal   rebellion   realm

1. kingdom _____realm_____

2. outcome decided ahead of time _____fate_____

3. living forever _____immortal_____

4. chosen by a vote _____elected_____

5. group of similar living things _____species_____

6. assigned or chosen by someone _____appointed_____

7. not able to be defeated _____invincible_____

8. uprising against the government _____rebellion_____

B **USING WORDS IN CONTEXT** Use the words in the box to complete the paragraph.

> acute   apprentice   myth   carriage   prosperous   timeless

There is a **(1)** _____myth_____ in my family about how my ancestors came to settle on this land. According to the story, my great-great-grandparents came to this area long ago. Everything they owned was on one horse-drawn **(2)** _____carriage_____ . After settling here, their young son, my great-grandfather became an **(3)** _____apprentice_____ to a local carpenter. Eventually he started his own business and became quite **(4)** _____prosperous_____ . Imagine how disappointed I was to learn that the story was all made up. The truth is that my parents moved to this town shortly before I was born!

© Great Source DO NOT COPY

Lesson 15 **57**

C **DEFINITIONS** Write the correct word from the box to answer each question.

| representative | abolish | realm | vertebrate | acute | responsive |

1. Which word best describes a very good sense of smell?
   _____acute_____

2. Which word describes human beings, whales, mice, and lions?
   _____vertebrate_____

3. Which word tells about reacting to something? _____responsive_____

4. Which word describes the land a king or queen rules?
   _____realm_____

5. Which word would you use if you wanted to get rid of something?
   _____abolish_____

6. Whom might you vote for? _____representative_____

D **USING CONTEXT** Each dictionary entry has several meanings. Use the sentence context to decide which meaning is correct. Then write the part of speech (noun, verb, or adjective) and the number of the correct definition.

vital *adjective* **1.** Of or relating to life: *The heart is a vital organ.* **2.** Necessary to life: *The heart and lungs are vital organs.* **3.** Very important; essential: *A good education is vital to a successful career.*

1. Your height and weight are **vital** statistics.
   part of speech _____adjective_____ definition number ___1___

2. Clean water was a **vital** supply for the astronauts.
   part of speech _____adjective_____ definition number ___3___

maul *noun* **1.** A heavy hammer, as one used for driving posts into the ground. Δ *verb* **1.** To injure by or as if by beating.

3. Our food tent had been **mauled** by the hungry bear.
   part of speech _____verb_____ definition number ___2___

4. Mrs. Jackson used a **maul** to split the wood for the campfire.
   part of speech _____noun_____ definition number ___1___

finish *verb* **1.** To bring or come to an end: *I have finished my lunch.* **2.** To use up. Δ *noun* **1.** The conclusion; end: *The finish of the relay race was very close.* **2.** The final treatment or coating of a surface: *The finish on the table top was smooth and shiny.*

5. At the **finish** of the swim meet, our school had won the most races.

   part of speech _____noun_____ definition number ___1___

6. The painter used a clear **finish** to protect the wood from rotting.

   part of speech _____noun_____ definition number ___2___

7. There was barely enough time for Ling to **finish** her dinner before she had to rush off to choir practice.

   part of speech _____verb_____ definition number ___1___

E **TEST-TAKING STRATEGIES** **Analogies** help you to use critical thinking skills. They also appear on many tests, so practicing them will make you a better test taker.

Page 19 has more information on working with analogies.

Strategy: The key to solving analogies is figuring out how the words are related. Three kinds of relationships are explained below.

- one word is a kind, or type, of another word (*cat* is a kind of *vertebrate*)
- one word is a synonym for another word (*acute* is a synonym for *sensitive*)
- one word is an antonym of another word (*spotless* is an antonym of *filthy*)

Directions: Write the word that completes each analogy on the line.

1. Hawk is to predator as chair is to _____furniture_____ .
   (*table/furniture*)

2. Carriage is to vehicle as soccer is to _____sport_____ . (*sport/cleat*)

3. Wrong is to mistaken as appointed is to _____assigned_____ .
   (*assigned/elected*)

4. Olfactory is to nose as auditory is to _____ear_____ . (*mouth/ear*)

5. Immortal is to mortal as addition is to _____subtraction_____ .
   (*math/subtraction*)

TEST-TAKING STRATEGIES On a **multiple-choice** test you are asked to choose an answer by filling in a "bubble." This exercise will give you practice with bubble answers.

Strategy: Read through the sentence and the answer choices. If there are choices that you are sure are *not* correct, skip those and focus on the remaining answers. When you select your answer, read the whole sentence through with your answer choice to make sure it is correct.

Directions: Fill in the bubble next to the word that best completes each sentence.

1. Rasheed learned to be a blacksmith by becoming a(n) _____ .
   (A) election (B) apprentice (C) immortal (D) vertebrate

2. The Greek _____ about Atlas carrying the world on his back is one of my favorites.
   (A) myth (B) realm (C) response (D) representative

3. *Charlotte's Web* is a(n) _____ tale about friendship and the circle of life.
   (A) elected (B) tactile (C) timeless (D) appointed

4. Becoming class president seemed to be Delia's _____ .
   (A) predator (B) species (C) carriage (D) fate

5. Many _____ of tree frog are found in the rain forests of South America.
   (A) responses (B) vertebrates (C) species (D) psyches

ENRICHMENT WORDS

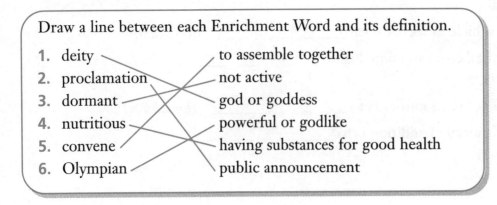

Draw a line between each Enrichment Word and its definition.

1. deity — to assemble together
2. proclamation — not active
3. dormant — god or goddess
4. nutritious — powerful or godlike
5. convene — having substances for good health
6. Olympian — public announcement

See page 129 for a reproducible test in standardized-test format.

FORMING NEW WORDS

Skill Lesson
prefixes and suffixes

In the next set of lessons, you will learn how to break apart words to find the meaning. You will also learn how to put word parts together to form new words. The key to this is understanding parts of words.

A **PREFIXES AND SUFFIXES** You have already learned about suffixes. A **suffix** is a group of letters attached to a root at the end. For example, in the word *slowly*, the root is *slow* and the suffix is *-ly*. When a suffix is written alone, it often has a line before it to show where the rest of the word attaches. Suffixes often change the number, tense, or the part of speech of a word.

Each of the words below has a suffix. Decide what the suffix is and write it after the word. The first one is done for you.

1. goodness _____-ness_____   4. hopeful _____-ful_____

2. opening _____-ing_____   5. endless _____-less_____

3. commented _____-ed_____

Another word part is called a **prefix.** This is a group of letters attached to the beginning of a word, before a root. At times, a prefix can also be just the first letters in a word. A prefix can give you important clues about the meaning of a word. Lessons 17, 18, and 19 will teach you important prefixes you can use in reading and writing. A prefix (like *sub-*) has a line after it to show where the root attaches.

One prefix you will learn is **sub-.** *Sub-* means "under" or "below." So when you come upon the word *subsoil* in your reading, you will know that it means "below the soil."

Another useful prefix to know is **super-,** which means "above," "over," or "very." Now that you know this, it is easy to figure out that a *superstructure* means a structure that is above or over another structure.

Point out that sometimes a prefix is attached to a word part that does not stand alone; for example, *superior.*

PREFIXES SUB- AND SUPER- Now see if you can use prefixes to determine the meaning of the boldfaced words in the following examples. Write the correct definition from the box to complete each sentence.

sub- = below or under   *super-* = above, over, or very

1. The **subarea** of a building is _____below or under_____ the main level.

2. A **supersharp** photograph is one that is _____very_____ clear.

3. A **subcommittee** works _____under or below_____ the main committee.

4. Your **superior** is someone who works _____over or above_____ you.

5. A **subcrustal** lava flow is one that is _____below or under_____ the earth's crust.

In the word *subarea* in example 1 above, it was easy to break down the meaning of the word by looking at its two parts: sub- + area = subarea. Sometimes a prefix is not attached to a whole word. In example 4, you can use the prefix *super-*, along with the sentence context and common sense, to help you figure out what *superior* means.

PREFIXES IN-, IL-, AND IM- There are other common and useful prefixes you can use to help you understand new words. One of these is *in-*, which means "not." It can also be spelled *il-* or *im-*. Here are some examples:

Inconsistent means not all the same, or not consistent.

Illegible means not clear, or not legible.

Impolite means rude, or not polite.

Write a definition for each boldfaced word.

1. **Inactive** means _____not active_____ .

2. **Inappropriate** means _____not appropriate_____ .

3. **Impractical** means _____not practical_____ .

4. **Immeasurable** means _____not measurable_____ .

5. **Improbable** means _____not probable_____ .

Lesson 17 teaches words with sub- and super-.

Lesson 18 teaches words with in-, il-, and im-.

improbable

62 Forming New Words

PREFIXES UNI-, BI-, AND TRI- The prefixes *uni-*, *bi-*, and *tri-* are also useful to know. *Uni-* means "one," *bi-* means "two," and *tri-* means "three." Here are some examples:

Lesson 19 teaches words with *uni-*, *bi-*, and *tri-*.

> A **unicycle** is a bike with <u>one</u> wheel.
> A **biweekly** magazine comes out every <u>two</u> weeks.
> A **triangle** has <u>three</u> angles.

Complete these examples that use the prefixes *uni-*, *bi-*, and *tri-*. Fill in the blank with the words *one*, *two*, or *three*.

1. A **triathlon** is a sporting event in which the athletes compete in
   _____three_____ different races.

2. A **unitard** is a leotard-and-tights set that is all _____one_____
   piece.

3. A **trimaran** is a sailboat with _____three_____ hulls side by side.

4. To **unify** is to bring together many pieces into _____one_____
   unit or whole.

5. Someone who is **bilingual** can speak _____two_____ languages.

6. **Bifocals** are glasses that have _____two_____ -part lenses.

7. A **unicorn** is a mythical beast with _____one_____ horn.

8. A **tripod** is a support with _____three_____ legs.

9. When you **bisect** something, you break or cut it into
   _____two_____ parts.

tripod

unicycle

USING PREFIXES The following sentences contain words in boldfaced type that you will be learning in the next few lessons. See if you can figure out what the boldfaced words mean just by looking at the prefixes and the roots. Use the words in the box to help you fill in the blanks.

---

sub- = under or below   *super-* = above, over, or very

in-, il-, im- = not   *uni-* = one

bi- = two   *tri-* = three

---

1. **Subterranean** means ____below or under____ the ground.

2. **Bicentennial** means occurring every _____two_____ hundred years.

3. **Immovable** means something is _____not_____ movable.

4. **Intolerable** means _____not_____ tolerable.

5. A **submarine** is a ship that floats ____under or below____ the water.

6. **Superheated** means _____very_____ hot.

7. A **trilogy** is a set of _____three_____ books, plays, or movies that go together.

8. **Unicellular** means having _____one_____ cell.

9. **Illegal** means _____not_____ legal.

10. **Subzero** means _____below_____ zero.

11. **Improper** means _____not_____ proper.

12. **Unique** means that it is _____one_____ of a kind.

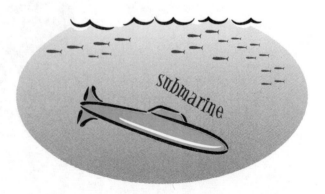

submarine

Under and Over
prefixes sub- and super-

A You will find the prefixes *sub-* and *super-* useful in your general reading and writing, and in studying science. The prefix *sub-* means "under" or "below"; the prefix *super-* means "above," "very," or "over." This lesson presents words with *sub-* and *super-*.

Have students draw a graphic that shows they understand the prefixes *sub-* and *super-*. For example, *sub-* might be shown underwater, with the top of the **b** sticking up like a periscope.

1. **submarine** (sŭb' mə rēn')
A **submarine** *is a ship that can go under water.* (noun)
In Jules Verne's novel *Twenty Thousand Leagues Under the Sea*, Captain Nemo explores the ocean in a **submarine.**

2. **submerged** (səb mûrjd') *Something that is* **submerged** *is entirely under water.* (adjective)
Entire houses were **submerged** during a terrible flood last spring.

3. **subservient** (səb sûr' vē ənt) *To be* **subservient** *is to be under another person's control; to be required to obey someone's orders.* (adjective)
In Greek mythology, humans are **subservient** to the gods.

4. **subterranean** (sub' tə rā' nē ən)
Something **subterranean** *is beneath the ground or hidden and secret.* (adjective)
Subterranean water in the Missouri Ozarks is home to two types of rare, blind, white crayfish.

5. **subzero** (səb zîr' ō) **Subzero** *means below zero.* (adjective)
We wore heavy coats walking in the **subzero** weather.

6. **superfluous** (sŏŏ pûr' flōō əs)
Something that is **superfluous** *is extra, or more than what is needed.* (adjective)
The extra scoop of ice cream on my cone was **superfluous** because I already had more than I could eat.

7. **superheated** (sŏŏ' pər hē' tĭd)
Something that is **superheated** *is very, very hot.* (adjective)
The volcano sent lava and **superheated** ash rolling down into villages.

8. **superimposed** (sŏŏ' pər ĭm pozd')
Something that is **superimposed** *has been placed over something else.* (adjective)
Some special effects are made when computer-created images are **superimposed** on a real background.

Draw a line between each vocabulary word and its definition.

1. subzero —————— below zero
2. subservient overheated
3. superheated underground
4. subterranean under orders

All the boldfaced words in the passage below include the prefixes *sub-* or *super-*. Read the passage. Then do the exercises that follow.

Bacteria Are Everywhere!

What can live in **subzero** ice packs, **submerged** in boiling water, and even without air? Why bacteria, of course! Although we often think of these one-celled life forms as agents of disease, bacteria can also help us.

We can thank bacteria for milk. One type lives in the largest of the cow's four stomachs. It takes the tough cover of grass, called *cellulose*, and changes it into food that the cow makes into milk. Other bacteria can then change the milk to yogurt.

Bacteria take elements in the air, such as carbon and nitrogen, and change them into forms that can be digested by living things. Far from being **superfluous,** bacteria are necessary to all life forms.

While some bacteria live on land, others inhabit the deepest **subterranean** recesses of the ocean, far beneath the ocean floor. Exploring with the aid of **submarines,** scientists have found bacteria in **superheated** vents that extend from the earth's center out to the ocean floor. These bacteria create food from the chemicals in the water.

Recently, explorers drilling for oil have found bacteria more than 1,500 feet under the ocean floor. They live under intense pressure, with no air. They survive on methane gas that is up to four million years old.

By taking advantage of their strange appetites, scientists have learned to use bacteria to clean up oil spills. Bacteria can be made **subservient** in this task by first feeding a diet of oil to a large sample of bacteria. Then, after a big oil spill, a layer of bacteria is **super-imposed** on the mess, and the bacteria eat the oil. The digested oil becomes harmless carbon dioxide and water.

WORD LIST

submarine

submerged

subservient

subterranean

subzero

superfluous

superheated

superimposed

1. What is one way that bacteria are helpful to humans?

   Bacteria play a role in making cow's milk, changing milk to yogurt, and
   cleaning up oil spills.

2. What are two places bacteria can live? What words tell you this?

   Bacteria can live in very cold ice packs (subzero), boiling water (submerged),
   and in deep, hidden parts of the ocean (subterranean).

C Break apart each word into its **prefix** and **root.** Write the prefix and root on the line, as shown in the example.

1. subservient = _sub- + servient_

2. subzero = _sub- + zero_

3. superheat = _super- + heat_

4. submarine = _sub- + marine_

5. superimpose = _super- + impose_

Remind students to break apart unfamiliar words into word parts they know.

D Choose the vocabulary word that best describes the situation in each sentence. Write the word on the line.

1. Heat a liquid to the boiling point without changing it into vapor.

   superheat *(submarine/superheat/superimpose)*

2. Place the image of the rainbow on top of the picture of the blue sky.

   superimpose *(superfluous/subservient/superimpose)*

3. The cave, deep in the earth, was dark, damp, and cool.

   subterranean *(submarine/submerge/subterranean)*

4. One kind of ship can work both on the water and beneath the water.

   submarine *(submarine/subservient/subzero)*

5. Renting both a movie and a video game for the evening was too much.

   superfluous *(subservient/superfluous/subterranean)*

E Complete each sentence with a phrase that makes sense. Note that another form of a vocabulary word has been used.

1. Crew members on a **submarine** should expect _____

_____ .

2. If you make a **subterranean** exploration, you go _____

_____ .

3. In **subzero** weather, you should wear _____

_____ .

4. To **submerge** something, _____

_____ .

5. A **subservient** person _____

_____ .

ENRICHMENT WORDS

Here are two more words that use the prefixes *super-* and *sub-*.
Try to figure out what they mean before you read the definitions.

See page viii for Enrichment Word Activities.

1. **superabundant** (sōō' pər ə **bun'** dant) **Superabundant** *means more than usual, too much.* (adjective)
   My puppy's **superabundant** energy tires me out.

2. **subculture** (sub' kŭl' chər) *A* **subculture** *is one part of a culture.* (noun)
   There are many different Native American **subcultures.**

OFF THE PAGE

Create a picture of **super-** and **sub-** words. Divide a piece of paper into a top half and a bottom half. Label the top half "Super Words." Label the bottom half "Sub Words." Write the vocabulary words in the proper half. Then think of other **sub-** and **super-** words to add. Draw pictures to help show the meanings of some of the words.

LESSON 18

"Not" Again!
prefixes in-, il-, im-

 Because it means "not," the prefix *in-* changes a word into an opposite. For example, *indirect* means "not direct." This prefix can be a bit tricky because it can be spelled three ways: *in-, il-,* and *im-*.

In a three-column chart write *illegal, immodest, intolerable*. Point out that the prefix in each word means "not." Head the columns with *il-, im-,* and *in-*. As you preview the words, add them to the proper column. Later, add more words that fit.

1. **illegal** (ĭ lē' gəl) *Something* **illegal** *is not lawful.* (adjective)
    It is **illegal** for cars to pass a stop sign without stopping first.

2. **illogical** (ĭ lŏj' ĭ kəl) *Something that is* **illogical** *does not make sense.* (adjective)
    It's **illogical** to think that the world is flat after pictures from the moon have shown it to be round.

3. **immodest** (ĭ mŏd' ĭst) *To be* **immodest** *is to show off; to be boastful.* (adjective)
    The **immodest** boy boasted about his good grades to his friends.

4. **immovable** (ĭ mōō' və bəl) *Something that is* **immovable** *cannot be moved or changed.* (adjective)
    The huge rock was **immovable.**

5. **immune** (ĭ myōōn') *To be* **immune** *from something is to be not affected by it or resistant to it.* (adjective)
    After you get chicken pox, you usually become **immune** to the disease and won't get it again.

6. **imperfection** (ĭm' pər fĕk' shən) *An* **imperfection** *is a flaw, or defect, that makes something not perfect.* (noun)
    A diamond with an **imperfection** is worth less than a perfect diamond.

7. **improper** (ĭm prŏp' ər) *Something* **improper** *is not suitable.* (adjective)
    It is **improper** to eat steak with your fingers.

8. **intolerable** (ĭn tŏl' ər ə bəl) *Something* **intolerable** *cannot be tolerated; it is unbearable.* (adjective)
    Lee found the violence in the video **intolerable,** so he turned it off.

Draw a line between each vocabulary word and its definition.

1. illegal — resistant
2. immune — flaw
3. intolerable — not bearable
4. imperfection — not lawful
5. improper — lacking modesty
6. immodest — not suitable

The boldfaced words in the passage below all contain prefixes meaning "not." Read the passage. Then answer the questions that follow.

Clothing in the Middle Ages

Do you have family members who constantly point out **imperfections** in your clothing? Have you ever been asked to leave a store because you weren't wearing shoes? If you find such things annoying, be glad you are not living in the Middle Ages, when there were laws about what kind of clothing people could wear.

In the Middle Ages, people were expected to dress according to their social class. People in power tried to keep the class system **immovable** by passing "Sumptuary Laws," which described proper and **improper** dress. It was particularly **intolerable** for middle- or lower-class people to wear expensive clothes or jewelry. This was considered most **immodest.**

In Bologna, Italy, the wearing of jewels, belts, embroidery, fur, dresses, and shoes was strictly limited. Laws were passed to specify the number of buttons that could be worn.

In England in the 1500s, it was **illegal** for everyone except kings and nobles to wear purple. Crimson, scarlet, and blue velvet could be worn by any noble, but not by commoners. These laws seem **illogical** to us today, but there may have been some practical purpose for them. For example, dyes were expensive. Of course, the queen stood above the laws and could, at any time, make her friends **immune** from them. Then they could wear as much red or purple as they wanted.

WORD LIST

illegal

illogical

immodest

immovable

immune

imperfection

improper

intolerable

1. What are some of the laws about clothing in the Middle Ages?

   People couldn't wear clothing with too many buttons, nor could

   they wear purple.

2. Why do the laws from the 1500s seem illogical to us today?
   Use at least two of the boldfaced words to explain.

   People have different ideas of what is improper or immodest.

C Choose the word that best completes each sentence. Write it on the line.

1. The sweater was on sale because there was an ___imperfection___ in the fabric. *(illegal/improper/imperfection)*

2. It is ___illegal___ to drive without a license. *(immovable/illogical/illegal)*

3. Vaccinations can make people ___immune___ to certain diseases, such as smallpox. *(immune/improper/immodest)*

4. It is considered ___improper___ to talk loudly in the library. *(imperfection/improper/illegal)*

5. The wall of sandbags was an ___immovable___ barrier that held back the raging river. *(intolerable/immovable/illogical)*

D Write a synonym from the word list for each pair of words.

1. nonsense, silly ___illogical___

2. unlawful, prohibited ___illegal___

3. flaw, mistake ___imperfection___

4. stuck, unchangeable ___immovable___

5. boasting, bragging ___immodest___

OTHER FORMS

illegally
illogically
immodestly
immunization
immunity
imperfect
improperly
intolerably
intolerant

E Complete each sentence with a phrase that fits. Note that some other forms of the vocabulary words are used in the sentences.

1. If someone is **illegally** parked, _____

_____ .

2. An example of an **immovable** object is _____

_____ .

3. Something I consider **intolerably** boring is _____

_____ .

4. An example of **improper** dress at a formal gathering would be

_____ .

5. An example of an **immodest** remark is _____

_____ .

Review with students how to break a word apart to understand its meaning. The words here have prefixes, suffixes, and roots.

ENRICHMENT WORDS

Here are two more words that have a prefix that means "not." Can you figure out their meanings without reading the definitions?

1. **impersonal** (ĭm pûr' sən əl) *Something that is* **impersonal** *shows no emotion or personality.* (adjective)

   The **impersonal** greeting read, "To whom it may concern."

2. **invariably** (ĭn vâr' ē ə blē) **Invariably** *means always.* (adverb)

   People **invariably** close their eyes when they sneeze.

See page viii for Enrichment Word activities.

OFF THE PAGE

Choose a vocabulary word. Then write a paragraph that compares the word with its base form. For example, you could compare **improper** dress at your school with proper dress. Or, you could compare something **illegal** with something legal.

One, Two, Three...
prefixes uni-, bi-, tri-

a biped

A Some prefixes give hints about word meanings by telling us about numbers. This lesson deals with common number prefixes. *Uni-* means "one," *bi-* means "two," and *tri-* means "three."

1. **unicellular** (yōō nĭ sĕl' yə lər) *A* **unicellular** *living thing has only one cell.* (adjective)
The amoeba is a **unicellular** organism.

2. **unique** (yōō nēk') *If something is* **unique** *there is nothing else like it; it is special.* (adjective)
Of all animals, human beings are **unique** in their language abilities.

3. **universe** (yōō' nə vûrs') *The* **universe** *consists of everything that exists, including stars and planets.* (noun)
Our **universe** contains the Milky Way, which has billions of stars.

4. **bicentennial** (bī' sĕn tĕn' ē əl)
A **bicentennial** *is the two-hundredth anniversary of an event.* (noun)
Ohio was admitted to the United States in 1803, so it celebrates its **bicentennial** in 2003.

5. **biped** (bī' pĕd') *A* **biped** *is an animal that walks on two feet.* (noun)
A bird is a **biped.**

6. **trilogy** (trĭl' ə jē) *A* **trilogy** *is a set of three books, plays, films, or stories that are related in subject or theme.* (noun)
What were the names of the three movies in the famous space film **trilogy?**

7. **triple** (trĭp' əl) *Something that is* **triple** *is three times as many; made up of three parts.* (adjective)
The champion ice skater could do **triple** axels, turning three times in the air.

8. **trivial** (trĭv' ē əl) *Something* **trivial** *is not important.* (adjective)
In ancient Rome people met to gossip, or talk about unimportant things, at a place where three roads met, so *tri* ("three") + *via* ("road") = **trivial.**

Draw a line between each vocabulary word and its definition.

1. biped — total existence
2. universe — one of a kind
3. unique — three times
4. triple — two-footed

The boldfaced words in the passage below all tell something about numbers. Read the passage. Then answer the questions that follow.

Dinosaurs—Gone, But Not Forgotten

Sixty-six million years ago, dinosaurs were kings of the earth. Although this **unique** animal species is gone, dinosaurs still fascinate us. One famous movie **trilogy** is based on the idea of a scientist who brings dinosaurs back to roam the world.

Some dinosaurs were huge. At about 50 feet tall, the Brachiosaurus was more than **triple** the height of a giraffe. Dinosaurs such as Tyrannosaurus rex, Gigantosaurus, and Carcharodontosaurus were the largest meat-eating animals that ever lived. One weighed almost two thousand pounds. But other dinosaurs were small. The Unenlagia was only four feet tall. Like a bird, it was a **biped** with hollow bones, but it probably could not fly.

Why did dinosaurs disappear? They didn't all die out at once. Different types of dinosaurs became extinct at different times. But all the dinosaurs that were alive 65 million years ago, as well as many other creatures, suddenly vanished. Many reasons have been put forth. One theory that is gaining popularity is that a huge asteroid traveling through our **universe** may have hit the earth. The effects of such an impact would not be **trivial**. It would have caused darkness and cold, acid rain, and huge forest fires, burning the dinosaurs, as well as many other species living on earth at that time. Although the largest life forms died out, the smallest, **unicellular** life forms were able to survive, perhaps underground.

The asteroid theory is supported by findings of iridium, a chemical common in outer space, and of soot, possibly from an explosion. In 1990, scientists looking for the depression that such a huge asteroid would create found one in Mexico, on the Yucatan Peninsula. Questions still remain, though—for example, Where did the asteroid come from?

The year 2018 will be the **bicentennial** of Solomon Ellsworth's important discovery of dinosaur bones. People were fascinated by these huge and mysterious bones. Two hundred years later, dinosaur bones and dinosaur mysteries continue to fascinate us.

WORD LIST

unicellular

unique

universe

bicentennial

biped

trilogy

triple

trivial

1. Use one of the boldfaced words to describe something we know about dinosaurs. _____
   Answers should reflect understanding of the chosen vocabulary word.

2. If Brachiosaurus was more than triple the height of a giraffe, about how tall is a giraffe? _____
   A giraffe must be about 16 or 17 feet tall, if 50 feet is three times its height.

C Replace the underlined word or phrase with a word from the list that has the same meaning.

1. Don't waste your time on <u>unimportant</u>, or _____trivial_____, pursuits.

2. A <u>one-celled</u>, or _____unicellular_____, organism is so small that it can only be seen through a microscope.

3. J.R.R. Tolkein wrote a popular <u>set of three books</u>, or _____trilogy_____, called *The Lord of the Rings*.

4. I've made a <u>one-of-a-kind</u>, or _____unique_____, necklace for my mother.

5. A big parade was planned to celebrate the town's <u>two-hundredth anniversary</u>, or _____bicentennial_____.

D List the words from the list above in the boxes in which they fit best. Then go back and add at least one more word using *tri-*, *bi-*, and *uni-* in each box.

Three	Two	One
trilogy	bicentennial	unicellular
triple	biped	unique
trivial		universe

Have students show a partner the words they added to the boxes. Then compile a class list. Words that students might add include *unicycle*, *unicorn*, *bicycle*, *bilingual*, *tricycle*, and *triangle*.

E Complete each sentence with a phrase that makes sense. Note that some other forms of the vocabulary words are used in the sentences.

1. A **biped** has _____

_____ .

2. If you **triple** your $5 allowance, you will have _____

_____ .

3. If you are **uniquely** qualifed to do something, _____

_____ .

4. If a person is **universally** admired, _____

_____ .

5. A **trilogy** has _____

_____ .

ENRICHMENT WORDS

Here are two more words that use a prefix that tells about number. If a bilingual person speaks two languages, how many languages would a trilingual person speak?

1. bilingual (bī lĭng' gwəl) *A* **bilingual** *person speaks two languages.* (adjective)

   Bernadette is **bilingual** in Tagalog and English.

2. triathlon (trī ăth' lən) *A* **triathlon** *is a long-distance race with three parts: running, swimming, and bicycling.* (noun)

   A person has to train for years to be ready to compete in a **triathlon.**

triathlon

OFF THE PAGE

Choose one of these topics to write about in a paragraph.

1. Describe a **triple** play in baseball.

2. What are three **trivial** ways to spend your time? For example, you might spend your time linking paper clips together in a chain.

20

Review
lessons 16–19

In this lesson, you will review the words and skills you have learned in the last four lessons. This will help you to remember them.

A **MATCHING WORDS AND DEFINITIONS**
Write the word from the box that matches each definition.

| subservient   immune   superfluous   improper   trivial   trilogy |

1. required to obey someone else _____subservient_____

2. resistant to or unaffected by _____immune_____

3. not suitable _____improper_____

4. more than is needed _____superfluous_____

5. unimportant _____trivial_____

6. a series of three _____trilogy_____

B **USING WORDS IN CONTEXT** Use the words in the box to complete the paragraph.

| submerged   intolerable   unique   immodest   universe   subzero |

   The life of an explorer is a **(1)** _____unique_____ one, for nothing is like it. I hope I am not being **(2)** _____immodest_____ when I say that I think I would make an excellent explorer. You see, I enjoy being in situations that others might find **(3)** _____intolerable_____ because they are so uncomfortable or even dangerous. One adventure might find me exploring sea life, **(4)** _____submerged_____ far below the surface of the ocean. Next, I might end up in the arctic, enduring **(5)** _____subzero_____ temperatures as well as complete isolation. As space travel becomes more common, I may be able to explore the far reaches of the **(6)** _____universe_____. Finally, I would settle down to write a book and let others know about the fun I had!

C **WRITING WORDS IN SENTENCES** Choose two of the words on each line to use in a sentence. You can change the form of the word if you like. (For example, *submerged* may be changed to *submerge*.)

1. **submerged   subterranean   superheated**

_____

_____

2. **submarine   imperfection   triple**

_____

_____

3. **bicentennial   improper   immodest**

_____

_____

4. **illegal   trivial   unique**

_____

_____

D **PREFIXES** Read the sentences below and determine the meaning from the **prefix** and the **context** of the sentence. Circle the letter of the word or phrase that best defines the word in boldface type.

1. Our firm's **biannual** meeting was a big success.

   A. occurring every year

   B. occurring every hundred years

   C. occurring twice a year

2. The scribbled letter was **illegible**.

   A. well-written

   B. clean

   C. not readable

3. An avalanche had made the ravine **impassable.**

   A. not scenic

   B. not able to be passed through

   C. worn and smooth

4. Gathering her courage, Rachel asked her **supervisor** for a raise.

   A. person who oversees another's work

   B. person who works for you

   C. person who works for another company

5. All the students answered the teacher in **unison.**

   A. immediately

   B. over again

   C. at one time

E **TEST-TAKING STRATEGIES** An **analogy** compares word pairs that are related in some way. An analogy can be expressed in a sentence or with colons (the single colon means "is to" and the double colon means "as").

Pages 19 and 59 have more information on working with analogies.

> *Superfluous* is to *extra* as *illegal* is to *unlawful.*
> Superfluous : extra :: illegal : unlawful

Strategy: To solve the analogies below, practice reading each one to yourself as a whole sentence, using the words "is to" and "as" in place of the colons.

Directions: Write the word that completes each analogy.

1. pleasant : intolerable : : immovable : _____flexible_____ *flexible/solid*

2. superimpose : overlap : : imperfect : _____flawed_____ *excellent/flawed*

3. submarine : submerge : : universe : _____unicellular_____ *triple/unicellular*

4. subzero : temperature : : illogical : _____answer_____ *warmth/answer*

5. lion : vertebrate : : bird : _____biped_____ *robin/biped*

F **TEST-TAKING STRATEGIES** On a **multiple-choice** test you are asked to choose an answer by filling in a "bubble."

Strategy: Read through the words and the answer choices. If there are choices that you are sure are *not* correct, skip those and focus on the remaining answers.

Directions: Fill in the bubble next to the word that gives the meaning of the underlined prefix.

1. <u>uni</u>cellular   <u>uni</u>verse
   - (A) not
   - (B) under
   - (C) one ●
   - (D) over

2. <u>im</u>mune   <u>im</u>perfection
   - (A) above
   - (B) three
   - (C) one
   - (D) not ●

3. <u>il</u>legal   <u>il</u>logical
   - (A) one
   - (B) not ●
   - (C) over
   - (D) under

4. <u>bi</u>centennial   <u>bi</u>ped
   - (A) one
   - (B) two ●
   - (C) three
   - (D) not

5. <u>sub</u>terranean   <u>sub</u>servient
   - (A) under ●
   - (B) over
   - (C) not
   - (D) two

6. <u>super</u>impose   <u>super</u>fluous
   - (A) very
   - (B) under
   - (C) three
   - (D) over ●

ENRICHMENT WORDS

Draw a line between each Enrichment Word and its definition.

1. superabundant — speaking two languages
2. subculture — showing no emotion
3. impersonal — three-part long-distance race
4. invariably — more than enough
5. bilingual — always
6. triathlon — part of a culture

See page 131 for a reproducible test in standardized-test format.

GOING BEYOND WORDS

Skill Lesson
using a thesaurus

The English language is rich in words that mean the same—or about the same—as other words. We have already learned that words that have the same meaning are called **synonyms.** For example, *big* and *large* are synonyms. A good place to find synonyms is in a **thesaurus.**

 USING THE THESAURUS When you find yourself using the same word too many times, make your writing more interesting by looking in a thesaurus to find other ways to say the same thing. Let's look at an example. Circle the word *big* each time it occurs.

> At the center of the circus was a big tent. All around it were big and small booths with games to play or trinkets to buy. Inside was a big circle where the animals and people performed. There was a dancing bear and some trick bicycle riders. Tim's favorite was a big elephant who stood on its hind legs and answered questions by nodding its head yes or no.

As a writer, you should vary your word choice. To do that, use a thesaurus. Here is the thesaurus entry for *big:*

> **big** *adjective* **1.** colossal, enormous, gigantic, huge, immense, large **2.** important, great, major, significant, vital

The thesaurus entry for *big* offers several words to choose from. But how do you choose? Many of the words a thesaurus gives mean about the same thing, but they differ slightly. These slight differences are called **shades of meaning.** You will learn some words with different shades of meaning in Lesson 22.

Notice that in the thesaurus entry for *big,* the words listed under 1 mean "big in size" and the words listed under 2 mean "big in importance." All the words mean *big,* but in slightly different ways.

Demonstrate how to look up a word in a thesaurus. Most children's thesauri are set up alphabetically, just like a dictionary.

Now let's improve the paragraph about the circus. Choose one of the words from the thesaurus entry for *big* to fill in each blank below. Think about whether you will choose from list 1 or list 2. Use a dictionary if you are not sure of the different shades of meaning.

There is more than one possible answer for each blank. Be sure that students use a synonym for big that makes sense in each blank.

At the center of the circus was a **(1)** _____ tent. All around it were **(2)** _____ and small booths with games to play or trinkets to buy. Inside was a **(3)** _____ circle where the animals and people performed. There was a dancing bear and some trick bicycle riders. The trick bicycle riders were a **(4)** _____ attraction. Tim's favorite was a **(5)** _____ elephant who stood on its hind legs.

B **SHADES OF MEANING** Here are some more examples of words that have different shades of meaning. Read each pair of words and write the one that best completes each sentence. Use a dictionary if you need help understanding the shades of meaning.

small   tiny

1. The _____tiny_____ insect could hardly be seen.

2. Jared hiked through the thick woods to a _____small_____ meadow.

bad   terrible

3. The sinking of the *Titanic* was a _____terrible_____ tragedy.

4. The chilly temperature and still air made it a _____bad_____ day for kite flying.

hill   mountain

5. David and Mercedes had an easy hike up the _____hill_____ .

6. The huge _____mountain_____ was like a wall between the two cities.

looked   peeked

7. The detective _____looked_____ at the clues for a long time before solving the case.

8. Janine quickly _____peeked_____ inside the mysterious box when she thought no one was watching.

C **USING A DICTIONARY** Now try these examples. Dictionary entries for two words appear above each pair of sentences. Think about the shade of meaning that the context of the sentence calls for. Then write the correct word to complete each sentence.

> **de-light-ful** (dĭ līt' fŭl) Greatly pleasing. *adjective*
>
> **good** (good̆) Having positive or desirable qualities; not bad or poor. *adjective*

1. Although it was old, the barn was still useable and in _____good_____ repair.

2. Meeting his favorite actor had been a _____delightful_____ surprise for Wyatt.

> **probe** (prōb) To investigate or explore. *verb*
>
> **ask** (ăsk) To put a question to. *verb*

3. Anisa did not want to _____ask_____ Hareem any more questions about the homework.

4. The commission decided to _____probe_____ into the cause of the accident.

> **meal** (mēl) The food served and eaten in one sitting. *noun*
>
> **feast** (fēst) A large elaborate meal, especially one prepared for a special occasion; a banquet. *noun*

5. This _____meal_____ was just like any other, as far as Sadie was concerned.

6. A large _____feast_____ was prepared in honor of the royal wedding.

feast

noise (noiz) Sound. *noun*

rack-et (răk' ĭt) A loud, unpleasant noise; uproar. *noun*

7. The only _____noise_____ they could hear was the low-level hum coming from the machinery.

8. "Now cut out that _____racket_____ !" Gina hollered at her brother.

an-gry (ăng' grē) Feeling or showing displeasure or hostility. *adjective*

fu-ri-ous (fyŏŏr' ē əs) Full of or marked by extreme anger; raging. *adjective*

9. Stefan was so _____furious_____ when he learned he had not made the team that he ran out of the gym, slamming the door behind him.

10. Keshia was more hurt than _____mad_____ when she found out she had not been chosen to represent her class at the science fair.

avoid (ə void') To keep away from; stay clear of. *verb*

shun (shŭn) To avoid deliberately and consistently. *verb*

11. Trying to _____avoid_____ looking in her eyes, Colby lied about the broken vase to his mother.

12. I am a loner and therefore _____shun_____ asking for help with anything.

D **REVISING A PARAGRAPH** Use the thesaurus entry below to revise the paragraph. Fill in each blank with an appropriate word for *darkness*.

darkness *noun* **1.** dimness, murk, blackness, gloom, gloominess **2.** dusk, evening, night, nightfall, nighttime

It was getting late. **Darkness** was everywhere. As the **darkness** fell, Julian could feel the **darkness** seep into his bones. **Darkness** would soon take over.

It was getting late. **(1)** _____ was everywhere. As the **(2)** _____ fell, Julian could feel the **(3)** _____ seep into his bones. **(4)** _____ would soon take over.

There are several correct answers for each blank. Be sure students vary the word choice to make the writing more specific. Have a few volunteers read their paragraphs aloud and discuss the effects of using different words.

Good or Bad?
shades of meaning

youthful

A Are you good at picking up hints? Some words hint at good or bad meanings. Such words are said to have *connotations*. All of the words below have good (positive) or bad (negative) connotations. As you study these words, think about the shades of meaning that were introduced to you in Lesson 21.

1. **observant** (əb zûr' vənt) *An* **observant** *person carefully notices things.* (adjective)
   Cheryl was so **observant** that she saw every tiny change in the ant farm.

2. **prying** (prī' ĭng) *A* **prying** *person snoops into things that should be private.* (adjective)
   The famous singer protects her family from **prying** reporters.

3. **youthful** (yo͞oth' fəl) *A* **youthful** *person is young and energetic.* (adjective)
   My **youthful** grandmother often goes in-line skating with me.

4. **immature** (ĭm' ə tyo͝or') *An* **immature** *person is childish and self-centered.* (adjective)
   My **immature** ten-year-old brother kicked the furniture in anger when he was not allowed to watch a movie.

5. **fearless** (fîr' lĭs) *A* **fearless** *person is brave and does not feel fear.* (adjective)
   George Washington was a **fearless** soldier who often led his men into battle.

6. **reckless** (rĕk' lĭs) *A* **reckless** *person is careless and takes stupid or silly risks.* (adjective)
   Two **reckless** drivers raced on a crowded highway.

7. **determined** (dĭ tûr' mĭnd) *Someone who is* **determined** *is serious and dedicated to achieving a goal.* (adjective)
   Mariah was **determined** to get an *A* on her science project.

8. **stubborn** (stŭb' ərn) *A* **stubborn** *person is not willing to give in or change.* (adjective)
   Jim isn't a good team member because he is so **stubborn** that he always wants to do things his way.

Draw a line between each vocabulary word and its definition.

1. youthful — careless
2. determined — young and energetic
3. reckless — dedicated
4. immature —— childish
5. stubborn — brave
6. fearless — unwilling to change

Review that some words have different shades of meaning. For example, the first two words both have to do with looking. *Observant* has a good meaning, but *prying* hints at something bad.

All the boldfaced words in the passage below have either positive or negative connotations. Read the passage. Then answer the questions that follow.

Dr. Sally Ride: Tennis Player, Astronaut, Professor

Dr. Sally Ride was the first American woman astronaut, but that was just one of her three career possibilities. One of her **youthful** interests was tennis. She played so well that tennis star Billy Jean King told her to become a professional. Instead, she decided to study physics at Stanford University. Sally was an excellent student, and was on her way to becoming a professor—until she learned that NASA was looking for astronauts.

NASA wanted intelligent astronauts who could also handle physical tasks. Another requirement was good judgment and the ability to follow orders. **Immature** or **stubborn** people can be dangerous on a space mission. NASA screened carefully, even asking questions that might be considered **prying,** but that were important in a life and death situation. In the end, Sally Ride was one of 35 people chosen out of more than 8,000 applicants.

Determined to excel, Ride trained in parachute jumping, water survival, and weightlessness. She was a **fearless** flyer who enjoyed being a pilot so much that it soon became her hobby. Ride became a radio communications specialist for the space mission. She had to be **observant** in monitoring her equipment so that nothing could go wrong, for communication with earth was critical to space missions. But Sally did other things too. She even helped design a remote mechanical arm.

Sally Ride went into space twice, and was preparing to go again when the *Challenger* space craft exploded. Shocked, the public demanded an explanation to see if any **reckless** act had caused the accident. Ride was appointed by the president to help investigate the disaster. Later she worked in NASA's Office of Exploration.

Dr. Ride has now retired from NASA and is a professor at Stanford University. One of her goals is to help young girls become interested in science and mathematics.

WORD LIST

determined

fearless

immature

observant

prying

reckless

stubborn

youthful

1. Which of Sally Ride's youthful accomplishments hinted that she would succeed as an astronaut? Why do you think so?

   Students' answers should be supported with details from the passage.

   _____

2. What words tell you about Sally Ride's qualities as an astronaut?

   She was determined and fearless.

   _____

C List the words from the word list in the boxes in which they fit best.

Good Connotations	Bad Connotations
determined	stubborn
youthful	immature
fearless	reckless
observant	prying

Have students also place these words in the proper columns: *consistent/monotonous, funny/silly,* and *clever/cunning.*

D Choose the right word to fit into each sentence. Write the word on the line.

1. I try not to ask _____prying_____ questions about other people's personal lives. *(observant/prying)*

2. Molly is so _____stubborn_____ that she won't listen to reason. *(stubborn/determined)*

3. If I were going to learn rock climbing, I'd want a _____fearless_____ instructor. *(reckless/fearless)*

4. Miguel's _____youthful_____ enthusiasm about dinosaurs was refreshing to the professor. *(immature/youthful)*

5. It's _____reckless_____ to try to feed bears in the wild. *(reckless/fearless)*

OTHER FORMS

determination

fearlessly

immaturely

observe

pry

recklessness

stubbornly

youthfulness

E Complete each sentence with a phrase that makes sense. Note that some other forms of the vocabulary words are used.

1. I marched **fearlessly** into _____

    _____ .

2. It is important to be **observant** when _____

    _____ .

3. When someone behaves **immaturely,** _____

    _____ .

4. It's not nice to **pry** because _____

    _____ .

5. If you are **determined** to do something, _____

    _____ .

ENRICHMENT WORDS

Here are two more words that have good and bad meanings. Which is the "good" word?

See page viii for Enrichment Word activities.

1. scholar (skŏl' ər) *A* **scholar** *is a learned person who has studied hard and gained a great deal of knowledge.* (noun)

    The **scholar** of ancient languages was called in to read the newly discovered Hieroglyphic scroll.

2. drudge (drŭj) *A* **drudge** *is one who works hard at doing boring and unpleasant work.* (noun)

    If you don't enjoy the work you are doing, you will feel like a **drudge** at the end of the day.

OFF THE PAGE

Choose one of the word pairs from this lesson, for example, **determined** and **stubborn.** Use examples from books, movies, and real life that show how the connotation is different for each word. For example,

Cinderella was determined to go to the ball.

Cinderella's step-sisters stubbornly refused to let her go.

determined

It's All Greek
words from ancient Greeks

A The ancient Greeks who lived more than 2,500 years ago had an important and advanced culture. The city of Athens was a center of learning, and Sparta was known for its attention to athletics. Many ancient Greek words are still used today.

1. **academic** (ăk' ə děm' ĭk) *Something* **academic** *refers to school subjects or knowledge.* (adjective)
In school we learn **academic** subjects, such as social studies and science, as well as other subjects, such as music and physical education.

2. **colossal** (kə lŏs' əl) *Something* **colossal** *is huge.* (adjective)
Colossal Mount Everest is the tallest peak on earth.

3. **Herculean** (hûr' ky lē' ən)
A **Herculean** *task requires great strength and effort.* (adjective)
With snow drifts piled up to twenty feet, plowing the sidewalks was a **Herculean** task.

4. **mentor** (měn' tôr') *A* **mentor** *is a wise, trusted advisor, counselor, or teacher.* (noun)
The basketball coach acted as a **mentor** to the girls on her team.

5. **Midas touch** (mī' dəs tŭch) *A person with a* **Midas touch** *makes money easily.* (noun phrase) People who have started Internet companies and made millions of dollars seem to have the **Midas touch.**

6. **odyssey** (ŏd' ĭ sē) *An* **odyssey** *is a long, adventurous journey.* (noun)
The long, dangerous boat trip was an **odyssey** of hope and courage.

7. **panic** (păn' ĭk) **Panic** *is a feeling of sudden and extreme fear.* (noun)
Her **panic** went away when she realized that she was being rescued from the stuck elevator.

8. **skeptical** (skěp' tĭk əl) *People who are* **skeptical** *are doubtful.* (adjective)
The teacher was **skeptical** when Taylor said the dog ate her homework.

Draw a line between each vocabulary word and its definition.

1. panic   doubtful
2. skeptical   long, adventurous trip
3. odyssey   feeling of fear
4. Herculean ——— requiring great strength
5. Midas touch   huge
6. academic   advisor
7. colossal   having to do with school subjects
8. mentor   creates wealth

Point out that the words in this lesson come from the Greek language and mythology. Explore ancient Greek myths and deities that students know.

B The boldfaced words in the passage below are about a very generous man named Albert Lexie. Read the passage. Then answer the questions that follow.

Albert Lexie: The Charitable Touch

It isn't hard to find Albert in the hospital—just ask for the shoeshine man. The **colossal** sums of money Albert Lexie has donated to sick children have made him famous in the Children's Hospital of Pittsburgh.

Albert Lexie's personal **odyssey** changed him from a person who needed help into a person who gives help. Born poor and developmentally disabled, he struggled hard in **academic** subjects. But, one day he saw some boys making shoeshine boxes in shop class. That's when he decided on his profession.

In 1979, Albert watched a telethon that was raising money for children's health care. Inspired, he decided that he would dedicate his life to this cause. Albert didn't have a **Midas touch;** in fact he earned less than ten thousand dollars that year. There was no **mentor** in Albert's life to show him how to raise money. But Albert had determination, and, through a **Herculean** effort, he raised more than seven hundred dollars to donate that year. A friend took him to visit the hospital he had helped, and the director offered him a job shining shoes for the staff.

All of Albert's tips go to help poor children who need medical services. Over the years, Lexie has donated over forty-four thousand dollars. His beloved mother has died, and he now lives in his own apartment. Although he may have been **skeptical** at first that he would be happy living alone, Albert now enjoys his independent life.

Albert is constantly in touch with others through his charity. He understands the **panic** a mother feels when she does not have enough money to help a sick child. Because of Albert Lexie's efforts, many of these children now receive medical care. Each month, he visits children in the hospital, and many have come to think of him as a role model.

WORD LIST

academic

colossal

Herculean

mentor

Midas touch

odyssey

panic

skeptical

1. Circle three boldfaced words in the passage that describe Albert Lexie. Then explain your choices on the lines below.

   Students might choose colossal, odyssey, Herculean, and skeptical.

   _____

2. How does Albert's income and life style form a contrast to the money he gives to charity?

   Albert is very generous with his money, but lives quite simply.

   _____

 Read about the history of the vocabulary words. Use the boldfaced clues to write the vocabulary word that fits. Then write what each word means now.

The Meaning Then	Vocabulary Word	The Meaning Now
1. **Odysseus** was a leader of the Greeks whose adventurous journey took ten years.	odyssey	long, adventurous journey
2. **Mentor** was a trusted advisor to Odysseus.	mentor	counselor, advisor
3. The **Colossus** of Rhodes was a statue so huge ships could pass between its legs.	colossal	huge
4. In Greek mythology, King **Midas** wished for everything he touched to turn to **gold.**	Midas touch	ability to make money easily
5. The Greek philosopher Plato **taught** at the **Akadēmeia.**	academic	having to do with school
6. **Hercules** was a Greek hero who had to do twelve difficult tasks to become immortal.	Herculean	requiring strength
7. **Skeptics** believed that real knowledge was impossible.	skeptic	doubtful
8. The god **Pan** (half human and half horse) produced a feeling of fear in humans.	panic	extreme, sudden fear

Point out that Midas touch and Herculean have kept the capitalization of their proper-name origins.

D Complete each sentence with a phrase that makes sense. Note that some other forms of the vocabulary words have been used.

1. If you had a **Midas touch**, _____

   _____ .

2. Sometimes people feel **panicky** when _____

   _____ .

3. My favorite **academic** subject is _____

   _____ .

4. I'm a real **skeptic** when it comes to stories about _____

   _____ .

5. I would like a **mentor** to help me learn _____

   _____ .

ENRICHMENT WORDS

Here are two more words that come from the Greek language. Try using these words in your conversation this week.

See page viii for Enrichment Word activities.

1. chaos (ka' os') **Chaos** *is a state of total disorder and confusion. Chaos comes from a Greek word that means "disorder of the universe."* (noun)

   A power failure left the city in **chaos.**

2. Spartan (spär' tn) **Spartan** *things are lacking in comfort or require self-discipline. The Greek city of Sparta was known for its training of athletes and warriors.* (adjective)

   The **Spartan** training program required soccer players to practice eight hours per day and get to bed by 7 P.M.

OFF THE PAGE

Something colossal is not just big, it's really, really big! Add three words of your own. It starts on the left with words that describe a small size and ends with the biggest of all—colossal—on the right.

Students can illustrate their word chain on poster board to emphasize the shades of meaning.

Miniscule ⇨ tiny ⇨ ⇨ 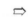 ⇨ colossal

LESSON 24

Great Advice
proverbs

A Has anyone ever said to you, "Birds of a feather flock together"? What a funny thing to say! In this case, the person means, "People who are alike enjoy being together." A proverb is a way of telling you a common truth. Which of these proverbs have you heard?

Read through the introduction. Find out whether students are familiar with these proverbs and whether they can think of any others.

1. A **proverb** is a short, common, wise saying that gives advice or states a rule about life. (noun)

2. **Birds of a feather flock together** means that people with similar personalities or interests tend to spend time together.

3. **Don't judge a book by its cover** means don't judge people or things by their appearances.

4. **Great oaks from little acorns grow** means that large or great things often start out small.

5. **Look before you leap** means you should consider carefully what might happen before you do something.

6. **Never leave till tomorrow that which you can do today** means do things as soon as you can.

7. **Small strokes fell great oaks** means steady, small actions will eventually accomplish something big.

8. **A stitch in time saves nine** means that if you repair things as soon as possible, you can avoid having to fix a bigger problem later.

Draw a line between each proverb and its explanation.

1. Never leave till tomorrow that which you can do today.

2. Birds of a feather flock together.

3. Great oaks from little acorns grow.

4. Look before you leap.

Think carefully.

Do it now.

Big things start out small.

Like attracts like.

Lesson 24 93

Name

Date

 The boldfaced proverbs are explained in the passage below. Read the passage. Then answer the questions that follow.

Words of Wisdom

Often, a **proverb** does not say directly what it means, but uses an example as a symbol. The proverb **"Small strokes fell great oaks"** creates a mental picture of someone chopping down a huge oak tree. Benjamin Franklin, the American who first published this proverb, wasn't talking about trees. Instead, he was saying that a big task is best completed by breaking it down into little parts.

In *Poor Richard's Almanack*, Franklin also wrote **"A stitch in time saves nine."** Picture a shirt with a tear in the sleeve. If you fix the hole right away it might take only one or two stitches; but if you wait, the hole may get bigger, and you will need to use many more stitches.

Some proverbs use observations about nature to make a point. "Birds of a feather," or birds of the same kind, such as crows or cardinals, do tend to stay together. **"Birds of a feather flock together"** can refer to groups of people who are alike in some way. **"Great oaks from little acorns grow"** is another observation that expresses a truth about life: small things can grow into large, important things.

Proverbs may offer practical advice, such as **"Don't judge a book by its cover."** A book with an exciting cover can turn out to be dull and boring. Likewise, a person who appears happy may really be sad inside. **"Look before you leap"** is a bit of practical advice that can be applied to many situations. Just as you wouldn't leap over a fence without checking what's on the other side, you shouldn't take an action without considering what may result. In Franklin's proverb, **"Never leave till tomorrow that which you can do today,"** Franklin used "today" to mean "as soon as possible." His advice to you would be to do your homework as soon as you get it!

1. Which two proverbs use trees as symbols?

   Small strokes fell great oaks. Great oaks from little acorns grow.

2. Choose two proverbs to encourage someone to start projects now rather than later. Circle them in the passage and explain your choices.

   Never leave till tomorrow..., A stitch in time..., Small strokes fell...,

   or possibly Great oaks... .

94 Going Beyond Words

© Great Source DO NOT COPY

Proverbs

Don't judge a book by its cover.

Never leave till tomorrow that which you can do today.

Birds of a feather flock together.

Small strokes fell great oaks.

Look before you leap.

Great oaks from little acorns grow.

A stitch in time saves nine.

C Write the proverb that best fits each example.

1. Forming an opinion of people by how they are dressed is not a good
   idea. For this reason, we say ___Don't judge a book by its cover.___

2. Have you ever noticed how people who like sports always seem to
   spend a lot of time together? This is what is meant by _____
   ___Birds of a feather flock together.___

3. When we realized that the huge company had started in the owner's
   garage, we thought ___Great oaks from little acorns grow.___

4. Your teacher assigned a project to be done over a week's vacation. It is
   Sunday night and you haven't started yet. If only someone had said to
   you: ___Never leave till tomorrow that which you can do today.___

5. Evan's room was a mess. It would be a big job to clean. The desk was
   covered with books and papers. Sports equipment was falling out of the
   closet. He would have to break the job apart and do a little at a time.
   ___Small strokes fell great oaks.___

6. A truth about life that is expressed in a sentence
   containing symbols is called a ___proverb___ .

Describe a situation in which you might use each proverb.

1. Look before you leap.

   Accept answers that show an understanding of each proverb.

2. Birds of a feather flock together.

3. Don't judge a book by its cover.

4. A stitch in time saves nine.

ENRICHMENT

1. **Beware of a wolf in sheep's clothing** *means watch out for people who seem friendly and harmless. They may actually intend to harm you.*

2. **The pen is mightier than the sword** *means people can be more truly conquered by persuasive words than by force.*

See page viii for Enrichment Word activities.

OFF THE PAGE

Make a poster for one of the proverbs in this lesson or one that you know. Illustrate the proverb exactly, but explain what the proverb really means. For example, on a poster for "A stitch in time saves nine," you might show a person sewing. Then you would add an explanation of the real meaning.

Review
Lessons 21–24

In this lesson, you will review the words and skills you have learned in the last four lessons. This will help you to remember them when you read and write.

A **MATCHING WORDS AND DEFINITIONS** Write the word from the box that matches each definition.

proverb academic odyssey stubborn youthful reckless immature fearless

1. young and energetic _____youthful_____
2. not willing to change _____stubborn_____
3. taking stupid risks _____reckless_____
4. having to do with school _____academic_____
5. wise saying _____proverb_____
6. brave _____fearless_____
7. long, adventurous journey _____odyssey_____
8. childish _____immature_____

B **USING WORDS IN CONTEXT** Use the words in the box to complete the paragraph.

panic mentor Herculean colossal odyssey skeptical

What began as a short trip to visit a favorite teacher, ended up being a month-long **(1)** _____odyssey_____ for Angela and Corinne. They had been in a **(2)** _____panic_____ because their community center did not have enough money to rent a bus for a field trip. With the advice of their **(3)** _____mentor_____ , Mr. Fukushima, however, they were soon on their way. He suggested they hold a car wash to raise money. At first Corinne was **(4)** _____skeptical_____ about the plan, but Angela soon convinced her it would work. It did seem like the fundraiser would take a **(5)** _____Herculean or colossal_____ effort, Angela agreed, but she thought they could do it. Sure enough, with Mr. Fukushima's help, the car wash was held within the month and was a **(6)** _____colossal_____ success!

PRACTICING PROVERBS Choose the saying from the box that best matches each situation. Write it in the space provided.

> **Don't judge a book by its cover.**
>
> **Great oaks from little acorns grow.**
>
> **A stitch in time saves nine.**
>
> **Look before you leap.**
>
> **Never leave till tomorrow that which you can do today.**

1. Everyone at the recital was amazed at how well Daniel played his piano piece. They all remembered that just two years ago he barely knew where to put his fingers.

   Saying: Great oaks from little acorns grow.

   _____

2. Mercedes was surprised to find that her birthday present was a beautiful, hand-painted ornament. She had not expected much because the gift box had been wrapped in plain, brown paper.

   Saying: Don't judge a book by its cover.

   _____

3. Nothing could be done about it. Jennifer had put all her money in the vending machine without bothering to read the "out of order" sign.

   Saying: Look before you leap.

   _____

4. Camila decided to R.S.V.P. to the party right away.

   Saying: Never leave till tomorrow what you can do today.

   _____

5. Putting tape around the weak parts of the splintery, old broom was a good idea. By doing that, Clarice was making sure it wouldn't break later—or give her a splinter—when she used it to sweep up the yard for the party.

   Saying: A stitch in time saves nine.

   _____

D **SHADES OF MEANING** This exercise helps you review the different shades of meaning in words. Remember that shades of meaning were discussed in Lesson 21 and in Lesson 22. Read each paragraph. Write the correct word in the blank to complete the sentence.

1. Shira always noticed the smallest details. When she went to visit her grandparents, she said, "Wow, you changed the furniture in the living room!" When she came back home, she noticed that her parents had gotten a new mailbox.

   The best word to describe Shira is _____observant_____ .
   (observant/prying)

Ask students to explain what clues they used to figure out the answers.

2. There was a lot of tension during the last game of the all-city basketball finals. The Tigers finally won by a two-point margin in overtime. After the game, to everyone's amazement, Tim, the center on the losing team, lay down on the gym floor and threw a tantrum.

   The best word to describe Tim is _____immature_____ .
   (youthful/immature)

3. The accident could have been avoided. Evidently, Joanne and Michael were having a contest as to who could bring their dirty dishes fastest to the dish-washing station in the cafeteria. That's when they ran into each other, breaking many dishes, as well as causing a few bruises.

   The best word to describe Joanne and Michael is _____reckless_____ .
   (fearless/reckless)

4. Everyone had agreed to the plan except Jill. Each player would take a turn at bat and then pitch the ball to the next batter. For some reason, Jill wouldn't go along. "I just don't feel like it," she whined.

   The best word to describe Jill is _____stubborn_____ .
   (determined/stubborn)

TEST-TAKING STRATEGIES Some **analogies** have word pairs that are synonyms. Some analogies have word pairs that are antonyms. Others go together in a "someone who" or "something that" relationship.

Strategy: Some analogy test items have a blank somewhere other than at the end. You use the same strategy to figure out the answer.

> human : mortal :: _____ : immortal
> (A) man   (B) woman   (C) Greek   (D) god

Read this item as, "A human is someone who is mortal and 'blank' is someone who is immortal." Choose the word that makes sense. (god)

Directions: Fill in the bubble next to the word that fits in each analogy.

1. busybody : prying : : _____ : observant
   (A) scientist   (B) microscope   (C) grandfather   (D) academic

2. stubborn : determined :: : _____ : thin
   (A) plump   (B) fearless   (C) well-fed   (D) emaciated

3. doubtful : skeptical : : _____ : panicky
   (A) Herculean   (B) wonderful   (C) risky   (D) fearful

4. father : parent : : _____ : advisor
   (A) hospital   (B) mentor   (C) school   (D) odyssey

5. colossal : tiny : : _____ : reckless
   (A) careful   (B) huge   (C) foolish   (D) neat

See page 133 for a reproducible test in standardized-test format.

ENRICHMENT WORDS

Draw a line between each Enrichment Word and its definition.

1. drudge — lacking in comfort
2. Spartan — a learned person
3. scholar — one who works hard at doing boring work
4. chaos — confusion
5. Beware of a wolf in sheep's clothing. — Written words are more effective than fighting.
6. The pen is mightier than the sword. — Watch out for people who seem friendly and harmless.

LOOKING INTO WORDS

Skill Lesson
prefixes, suffixes, and roots

A **PREFIXES, SUFFIXES, ROOTS** Three word parts that help you with meaning are **prefix, root,** and **suffix.** A **prefix** comes before a root and affects its meaning. A **root** is the main meaning of the word. Some roots are words and some are not. A **suffix** comes after a root and often changes the number, tense, or part of speech of a word.

The word **disconnecting** has a prefix, a root that is a word, and a suffix. Look for the dashes that show where the prefix and suffix attach to the word.

> prefix **dis-**   root **connect**   suffix **-ing**

The word **distracted** has a prefix, a root that is *not* a word, and a suffix. Again, look for the dashes. Notice that the root, **tract,** cannot stand alone as a word.

> prefix **dis-**   root **tract**   suffix **-ed**

disconnecting

Now let's practice dividing words into prefixes, roots, and suffixes. Write the prefix, root, and suffix for the words below. In this exercise, all the roots are words. Remember to use dashes in the right place. The first one has been done for you.

WORD	PREFIX	ROOT	SUFFIX
disarrangement	dis-	arrange	-ment
disappearance	dis-	appear	-ance
transplanting	trans-	plant	-ing
dishonesty	dis-	honest	-y
amphitheaters	amphi-	theater	-s

PREFIXES In the next three lessons, you will be learning more prefixes. These prefixes and their meanings are listed below.

Prefix	Meaning
dis-	opposite, not
trans-	across, go across
ambi-, amphi-	both, around
circu-	around

Now try some examples with *dis-*. Write the meaning of the prefix in each blank.

order

1. *Disorder* means __the opposite of__ order.

2. *Discomfort* means __the opposite of__ comfort.

3. *Dishonesty* means __the opposite of__ honesty.

disorder

The above examples were fairly simple to figure out because the roots were words. But sometimes a root that is *not* a word is used. In this case, you can still use the prefix—along with the context—to help you understand the meaning of an unknown word. For example, look at the word *disturb* in the following sentence.

 The noise of the bulldozer working next door gradually began to <u>disturb</u> Harry's sleep.

You do not have to know the meaning of the root *turb* to understand that Harry could not continue sleeping.

Lesson 27 has words with the prefix dis-.

 PREFIX *TRANS-* Now try some examples with *trans-*. Write the meaning of the prefix ("across" or "go across") in the blanks below.

1. The **transcontinental** railroad reaches __across__ the continent.

2. A radio **transmission** travels __across__ the air waves to a receiver.

3. An airplane flight that __goes across__ an ocean is called **transoceanic**.

D **PREFIXES AND ROOTS** Sometimes a root that is not a word is used with *trans-*. In this case, just combine the meaning of *across* with the sentence context to figure out the word.

> **Translate** means to express in a different language, or to go "across" languages.
>
> **Transfer** means to move from one place to another, or to go "across" places.
>
> A **transplant** takes something from one place and plants, or puts it, somewhere else, or "across" places.

At times, rather than meaning *across*, the prefix *trans-* may include the idea of movement or change. In the word **transform,** for example, we change forms, or "move across" forms. In the following examples, use your knowledge of the prefix *trans-*, along with the context and your common sense, to figure out the meaning of the boldfaced words.

Lesson 28 has words with the prefix *trans-*.

1. After emerging from the cocoon, it was obvious that the caterpillar had been **transformed** into a butterfly.

    Transformed means _____changed_____ .

2. After losing so much blood in the car accident, the patient needed a blood **transfusion.**

    Transfusion means _____move across_____ .

3. Trains, trucks, ships, and airplanes are all ways to **transport** goods to stores.

    Transport means _____carry across_____ .

PREFIXES *AMBI-* AND *AMPHI-* Some prefixes have more than one meaning. *Ambi-* and *amphi-* may mean "both" or "around." When you come upon a new word with the prefix *ambi-* or *amphi-*, for example, you may have to try out both meanings to see which makes the most sense. Once again, you can use context clues and your common sense. In each sentence below, write *both* or *around* to complete the sentence.

1. Someone who is **ambidextrous** can write equally well with

   _____both_____ hands.

2. **Amphibians** are animals that live _____both_____ on land and

   in water.

3. To **amble** from place to place is to walk _____around_____ slowly.

4. An **amphitheater** has rows of seats rising _____around_____ an

   open space at the center.

Lesson 29 has words with prefixes *ambi-*, *amphi-*, and *circu-*.

 WORD PART *CIRCU-* In these words, *circu-* means "around." *Circu-* is usually a prefix. Sometimes it is a root, as it is in the word *encircle*.

1. Your **circulatory system** pumps blood _____around_____ your

   body.

2. **Circumlocution** is talking _____around_____ a topic, but never

   getting to the point.

3. To **circumnavigate** the globe is to sail _____around_____ the world.

4. To **circumvent** the law is to try to get _____around_____ it.

circumnavigate

Opposite "Dis-"
prefix dis-

disaster

A The prefix *dis-* means "not" or "opposite." The words below all include this prefix. You will find this prefix in many words, so studying words with *dis-* will help you in reading and writing.

1. **disadvantage** (dĭs' əd văn' tĭj)
   A **disadvantage** *is an unfavorable condition; a condition that makes something harder.* (noun)
   It can be a **disadvantage** to be short if you want to be a basketball star.

2. **disagreeable** (dĭs' ə grē' ə bəl)
   Something **disagreeable** *is unpleasant.* (adjective)
   Skunks produce a very **disagreeable** odor when they are frightened.

3. **disaster** (dĭ zăs' tər) *A* **disaster** *is a calamity or terrible event that causes suffering.* (noun)
   The sinking of the *Titanic* was a **disaster** that killed many people.

4. **discharge** (dĭs chärj') *To* **discharge** *is to release, get rid of, or send away.* (verb)
   Doctors will **discharge** the patient from the hospital two days after the operation.

5. **discomfort** (dĭs kŭm' fərt)
   Discomfort *is the opposite of comfort or ease.* (noun)
   The hard, lumpy seats caused great **discomfort** for the audience.

6. **discontent** (dĭs' kən tĕnt')
   Discontent *is a feeling of not being happy or satisfied.* (noun)
   Students voiced their **discontent** with the long lines in the school cafeteria.

7. **discouraged** (dĭ skûr' ĭjd)
   When people become **discouraged,** *they lose hope or confidence.* (adjective)
   When she saw how fast her opponents ran, Marla became **discouraged** and quit the race.

8. **disgrace** (dĭs grās') *A* **disgrace** *is a loss of honor or respect; a disgrace brings shame.* (noun)
   The mayor left office in **disgrace** when he was found guilty of stealing city money.

Draw a line between each vocabulary word and its definition.

1. disgrace   terrible event
2. discharge   lack of ease
3. discomfort   unpleasant
4. disaster   shame
5. disagreeable   release

Discuss the popular use of the term *dis*, as in "Don't dis me!" Elicit that *dis* is short for *disrespect*. Point out that the prefix indicates a lack of something, something negative. Have students brainstorm *dis-* words that they know.

All the boldfaced words in the passage below include the prefix *dis-*. Read the passage. Then answer the questions that follow.

Stagecoaches: Romance or Discomfort?

Does traveling by stagecoach sound exciting to you? During the 1800s, stagecoaches carried passengers to the West. With luck, a trip from Missouri to California took twenty days. Inside the stagecoach, six passengers sat on benches. On long trips, a passenger might be stuck next to a boring or **disagreeable** person for several days.

As the coach swayed back and forth, people often experienced the **discomfort** of motion sickness. In spring and fall, coaches rode through mud. In winter, the uneven frozen tracks bounced passengers several feet into the air.

Many stagecoaches traveled day and night. It was difficult for people to sleep because of the big bounces on rough dirt roads. If a coach was stuck in mud, the passengers had to get out and push. If horses were injured, someone walked to the nearest stagecoach station for help. **Disaster** was always possible.

A few coaches went off cliffs in the dark of night. Others were robbed.

The coach stopped for meals, but passengers often had to eat very quickly. Naturally, this led to much **discontent.** Some passengers became **discouraged** about completing the trip. When the coach **discharged** passengers for dinner, they might decide not to get back on.

In contrast, the drivers were tough and determined. They considered it a personal **disgrace** if their stagecoaches did not finish the trip safely. Yet, as hard as they tried, it was difficult to go more than fifteen miles per hour.

With all of these **disadvantages,** people were anxious for other ways to get to the West. As the railroads reached more areas, stagecoaches rapidly disappeared.

WORD LIST

disadvantage

disagreeable

disaster

discharge

discomfort

discontent

discouraged

disgrace

1. What was it like to travel by stagecoach? Use at least two vocabulary words in your answer. _____

   Students might describe travel as disagreeable and causing discomfort.

2. What were two of the disasters that could happen during stagecoach travel? _____

   Examples of disasters are going off a cliff and being robbed.

C Underline the word in each row that is a synonym for the boldfaced word.

1. **discontent**   joy   <u>unhappiness</u>   fear
2. **disgrace**   honor   bore   <u>shame</u>
3. **discharge**   <u>release</u>   welcome   bring
4. **disagreeable**   fun   <u>unpleasant</u>   correct
5. **disaster**   flower   destination   <u>tragedy</u>

D Remember that *dis-* means "opposite." Fill in the blanks below by choosing the correct word. This exercise will help you to understand the prefix *dis-* and how it is used with roots.

1. An **agreeable** person is easy to get along with. A **disagreeable** person is the _____opposite_____ *(opposite/across)*. Here *dis-* is a _____prefix_____ *(suffix/prefix)* that is added to the root **agreeable.**

2. A person who is **encouraged** thinks good things will happen. A person who is **discouraged** thinks _____bad_____ *(good/bad)* things will happen. An **encouraged** person could be said to be "filled with" courage. A **discouraged** person could be said to be _____emptied of_____ *(emptied of/helped by)* courage.

3. The ancient Greeks felt that the stars brought good luck. Their word for stars sounded like *aster.* In the word **disaster,** the prefix is _____dis-_____ *(dis-/aster).* The prefix plus the root mean "the _____opposite of_____ *(same as/opposite of)* good luck."

OTHER FORMS

disadvantageous
disagreeably
disagreement
discomforting
discontentment
disgraceful
disgracefully

E Complete each sentence with a phrase that fits. Note that some other forms of the vocabulary words have been used.

1. **Discontentment** can lead to _____

_____ .

2. Something that causes great **discomfort** is _____

_____ .

3. It's **disgraceful** to _____

_____ .

4. When you feel **discouraged,** _____

_____ .

5. An example of a **disagreeable** sight is _____

_____ .

See page viii for Enrichment Word activities.

ENRICHMENT WORDS

Here are two more words that have the prefix *dis-*.

1. **disintegrate** (dĭs ĭn' tĭ grāt') *To* **disintegrate** *is to fall apart or become worse; the opposite of integrate.* (verb)

Old paper can **disintegrate** into powder if it becomes too dry.

2. **disclose** (dĭs klōz') *To* **disclose** *means to let out a secret or to uncover.* (verb)

Tomorrow, the judges will **disclose** who won the contest.

OFF THE PAGE

Choose two vocabulary words from the lesson. First use each word in a sentence. Then take off the prefix *dis-* and use the remaining words in their own sentences. Here's an example.

The smell of trash can be disagreeable.

The smell of cooking food can be agreeable.

LESSON 28

Across the Way
prefix trans-

A The prefix *trans-* means "across" or "go across." At times it can also mean "movement" or "change." The words below all include *trans-*. Try to figure out what *trans-* means in each word.

Write *transcontinental* so that everyone can see it. Ask students to underline smaller parts of the word to figure out what this word means. Guide them to identify the main parts *trans* and *continent*. Review that some words have roots that are words, like *continent,* and others have roots that are not words (see *transition*).

1. **transaction** (trăn săk' shən) *A* **transaction** *is an act, especially business, done between, or "across," people.* (noun)
   The **transaction** was complete when both parties signed the documents.

2. **transcontinental** (trăns' kŏn tə něn' tl) **Transcontinental** *means crossing a continent.* (adjective)
   We took a **transcontinental** flight from Los Angeles to New York.

3. **transform** (trăns fôrm') *To* **transform** *something is to change its form or appearance.* (verb)
   It's exciting to see a tadpole **transform** into a frog.

4. **transfusion** (trăns fyoo' zhən) *A* **transfusion** *is the transfer of something, such as blood, from one person or thing into another.* (noun)
   Before you receive a **transfusion** of blood, check your blood type.

5. **transition** (trăn zĭsh' ən) *A* **transition** *is the process of passing, or going across, from one activity or place to another.* (noun)
   Serena made the **transition** from her old school to her new one easily.

6. **translate** (trăns' lāt') *To* **translate** *means to take something from one language and express it in another.* (verb)
   My grandmother speaks only Greek, so I **translate** her words into English for my friends.

7. **transplant** (trăns plant') *To* **transplant** *is to move something that is planted in one place to another place.* (verb)
   We decided to **transplant** the rose bush from our old house to our new house.

8. **transport** (trăns pôrt') *To* **transport** *means to carry something from one place to another.* (verb)
   The truck driver will **transport** the peaches from South Carolina to New York.

Draw a line between each vocabulary word and its definition.

1. transport — express in another language
2. transplant — from one activity to another
3. translate — carry from one place to another
4. transition — uproot and plant elsewhere

The boldfaced words in the passage below all contain the prefix *trans-*. Read the passage. Then answer the questions that follow.

Transplants: Modern Medical Miracle

Just fifty years ago, a child with inherited lung or kidney disease would probably have died before reaching adulthood. But today, we can **transplant** organs from one person to another and save many lives. A precious organ may even make a **transcontinental** journey to reach the person who needs it.

Suffering from cystic-fibrosis, teenager Andrew Croy waited for new lungs. Armed with a pager, he was ready to go into surgery at a moment's notice. Finally, a national network found a donor's lungs and called Andrew's hospital. If Andrew did not accept the donation within one hour, the lungs would have to be given to someone else. The hospital paged Andrew only to find that his beeper was out of order! Frantically, they called his mother, located him at a hockey game, and got him to the hospital with only fifteen minutes to spare. Meanwhile, a medical team flew to the donor's hospital to pick up the lungs and **transport** them to Andrew. Soon, Andrew was on the operating table, with blood supplies ready in case a **transfusion** was needed. The entire **transaction** took only a few hours. Today, Andrew's life has been **transformed** by his new, healthy lungs. He now can live normally, without fear of life-threatening infection.

Transplants have saved thousands of lives. Like Andrew, many people have been able to make the **transition** from illness back to health. In today's world, a person's signature on a card that allows organs to be given to another person **translates** into the gift of life.

1. How was Croy's life transformed by the operation?

   The healthy lungs allowed Croy to live a normal life.

2. Explain how each of the three words below are involved when a doctor transfers an organ from one person to another: **transport, transplant, transfusion.**

   First, one has to transport the organ, then prepare for a blood transfusion, and

   finally transplant the organ.

WORD LIST

transaction

transcontinental

transform

transfusion

transition

translate

transplant

transport

C Choose the vocabulary word that best completes each sentence. Write the word on the line.

1. We took a ___transcontinental___ flight from Morocco in northern Africa to South Africa. *(transcontinental/transform/transfusion)*

2. It's difficult to ___transport___ large packages on a bicycle. *(translate/transition/transport)*

3. I'm planning to ___transform___ this piece of junk into a work of art. *(transport/transaction/transform)*

4. When you ___transplant___ a rose bush, put a banana peel in the new hole to give the plant extra potassium and improve its growth. *(transplant/transaction/transition)*

5. When you ___translate___ from one language to another, you need to be careful to keep the original sense of what was said. *(transfusion/transport/translate)*

D Remember that *trans-* usually means "across" or "go across." At times it can also mean "movement" or "change." Fill in the blanks below by choosing the correct choice.

1. A **transaction** is an action that goes ___across___ *(opposite/across)* people. The root in this word is ___action___ *(action/trans-)*.

2. When we **transform** something, we ___change___ *(around/change)* it from one form to another. In this word, the root ___is___ *(is/is not)* a word.

3. When we **translate** something, it goes ___across___ *(across/opposite)* languages. We know this because the ___prefix___ *(prefix/suffix)* is *trans-*.

transaction

OTHER FORMS

transact

transformation

transfuse

translation

translator

transportation

E Complete each sentence with a phrase that makes sense. Note that some other forms of the vocabulary words are used.

1. My favorite form of **transportation** is _____

_____ .

2. A person might need a **transfusion** if _____

_____ .

3. I would like to **transform** the playground into _____

_____ .

4. The **transition** from our old house to our new house _____

_____ .

5. The job of a **translator** might be to _____

_____ .

ENRICHMENT WORDS

Here are two more words that begin with the prefix *trans-*. How many other words can you list?

See page viii for Enrichment Word activities.

1. **transitory** (tran' si tôr' e) *Something that is* **transitory** *lasts for only a short time; it passes quickly.* (adjective)

   Maria's wish for a dog was **transitory;** the next week she wanted a cat.

2. **transpose** (trans pōz') *When we* **transpose** *things, we reverse their positions.* (verb)

   I accidentally **transposed** 43 by writing it as 34.

transcontinental

OFF THE PAGE

Write about a transcontinental trip you might take. You may choose to cross any of the seven continents. Be specific about where you will go, how you will travel, and what sights you will see.

LESSON 29

Around and Around
word parts ambi-, amphi-, circu-

A The prefixes *ambi-* and *amphi-* mean "both" or "around." *Circu-* means "around." The words below include these word parts. As you study the words, think about what the word part means in each one.

Amble, circulate, and *encircle* are three verbs from this list that can be demonstrated. Have a student study the definition for each word and act out the word.

1. **ambition** (ăm bĭsh' ən) **Ambition** *is a desire to achieve or do something.* (noun).
   His **ambition** to become a pilot led him to take flying lessons.

2. **amble** (ăm' bəl) *To* **amble** *is to walk around slowly.* (verb)
   We like to **amble** through the park, enjoying the trees.

3. **amphibian** (ăm fĭb' ē ən) **An amphibian** *is an animal that lives both on land and in water.* (noun)
   A frog is an example of an **amphibian.**

4. **circuitous** (sər kyōō' ĭ təs)
   A **circuitous** *route is not direct, but is roundabout.* (adjective)
   Since Tom wasn't in a hurry to get to school, he took a **circuitous** route, stopping at several places that were out of the way.

5. **circulate** (sûr' kyĕ lāt) *To* **circulate** *is to move around in a circle.* (verb)
   Blood **circulates** through the human body, supplying it with oxygen.

6. **circumference** (sər kŭm' fər əns)
   The **circumference** *is the distance around a circle.* (noun)
   The **circumference** of the earth is about 25,000 miles.

7. **cycle** (sī' kəl) *A* **cycle** *is a series of events that repeats, or goes around, many times.* (noun)
   The **cycle** of seasons—winter, spring, summer, and fall—repeats each year.

8. **encircle** (ĕn sûr' kəl) *To* **encircle** *is to put a circle around.* (verb)
   To protect their camp, the settlers would **encircle** it with their wagons.

Draw a line between each vocabulary word and its definition.

1. circulate   strong desire
2. encircle   repetition of events
3. ambition   move around
4. cycle   put a circle around
5. circuitous   lives both on land and in water
6. amphibian   not direct

circumference

The boldfaced words in the passage below have the word parts *ambi-*, *amphi-*, or *circu-*. Read the passage. Then answer the questions that follow.

Croaking Frogs Mean a Healthy Environment

Three times each year, a group of people from Chicago follow a **circuitous** path through parks, lawns, and roadsides. As they go, they listen for the sounds of frogs. Their **ambition** is to count and classify each one. As they **amble** around the **circumference** of a park, they might hear the musical trill of an American frog or the deep croak of a bull frog. More croaks mean more frogs.

In recent years, scientists have noted a steep decrease in the number of frogs and other **amphibians** such as toads, salamanders, and newts. This may be an early warning of trouble in the environment. Amphibians are very sensitive to environmental changes.

What could be going wrong? One problem may be a thinning of the ozone layer that **encircles** the earth. The thinner layer lets in too much ultraviolet light for frog eggs. This kills the frog at the earliest part of its life **cycle.** Researchers found that eggs protected from the sun's rays hatched much better than unprotected eggs.

Another problem may be a newly discovered virus, found on the skin of frogs. Strangely, this may be caused by human beings who are trying to protect frogs. As scientists **circulate** through frog habitats in an effort to study them, they may be accidentally spreading the virus.

Whatever the cause, we need to protect the world's frogs. Across the world, volunteers and professionals are listening to frog croaks and researching ways to help this precious part of the environment.

1. Describe one change that could be affecting the amphibian population.

   One change is the thinning of the ozone layer, which affects how the eggs

   hatch. Another change is a virus that may be spread by humans.

2. Why do the people follow a circuitous route?

   Because by walking around, they can cover as much ground as possible and

   have the most opportunities to hear frogs.

C Circle the word that best completes each sentence.

1. Let's (*encircle*   *circulate*   (*amble*)) down to the river bank.

2. To secure the back yard, (*cycle*   (*encircle*)   *ambition*) it with a fence.

3. Elena's (*amphibian*   (*ambition*)   *cycle*) is to become a doctor.

4. ((*Circuitous*)   *Circumference*   *Encircle*) is the opposite of *direct*.

5. A(n) ((*amphibian*)   *ambition*   *circumference*) is a cold-blooded animal.

D *Ambi-* and *amphi-* mean "both" or "around." *Circum-* means "around." Fill in the blanks below by choosing the correct word or phrase.

1. In the word **circumference** the prefix *circum-* means _____around_____ (*around/both*). The root *ference* _____is not_____ (*is/is not*) a word. In the word **amphibian,** the prefix *amphi-* means _____both_____ (*around/both*).

2. At times, a word part changes its spelling when it is put into a word. The words **cycle** and **encircle** contain the word part _____circum-_____ (*ambi-/circum-*), but it is spelled differently in these words. When *circum-* is used as the prefix of the word, it comes _____before_____ (*before/after*) a root.

3. In ancient Rome, people who wanted to be elected for an office were called **ambitious** because they went _____around_____ (*around/both*) the town looking for votes.

OTHER FORMS

ambitious

amphibious

circuit

circulation

recycle

E Complete each sentence with a phrase that fits. Note that other forms of the vocabulary words are used in some sentences.

1. Someone who is **ambitious** _____

_____ .

2. An example of an **amphibious** animal is _____

_____ .

3. When you **recycle,** _____

_____ .

4. A fan **circulates** air by _____

_____ .

5. If you **amble** along, you _____

_____ .

ENRICHMENT WORDS

Here are two more words that use the word parts *ambi-* and *circum-*. Do you know anyone who is ambidextrous?

See page viii for Enrichment Word activities.

1. **ambidextrous** (am' bi **dek'** strəs) *An* **ambidextrous** *person can use right and left hands equally well.* (adjective)

   In 1995, **ambidextrous** baseball player Greg Harris used both his right hand and his left hand to pitch in the same game.

2. **circumvent** (sûr' kəm **vent'**) *When we* **circumvent** *something, we avoid it or go around it.* (verb)

   Some people use e-mail to **circumvent** the problem of slow mail delivery.

OFF THE PAGE

Do a word web for the word **cycle.** Write the word *cycle* in the middle of a piece of paper. Circle it. All around the circle, write words that have the word *cycle* as the root. List at least four words besides *recycle.* Use a dictionary, if you wish.

See page xii for a word web.

recycle

cycle

Review
Lessons 26–29

In this lesson, you will review the words and skills you have learned in the last four lessons. This will help you to remember them when you read and write.

A MATCHING WORDS AND DEFINITIONS
Write the word from the box that matches each definition.

> cycle discouraged transaction encircle disgrace
> ambition transition discharge

1. loss of honor or respect _____disgrace_____
2. desire to achieve or do something _____ambition_____
3. carrying out a business action between people _____transaction_____
4. passage from one activity to another _____transition_____
5. a series of events that repeats _____cycle_____
6. to put a circle around _____encircle_____
7. without hope or confidence _____discouraged_____
8. to release or send away _____discharge_____

B USING WORDS IN CONTEXT Use the words in the box to complete the paragraph.

> transporting circuitous discomfort circulate disaster disagreeable

The Sanchez family vacation had nearly been a **(1)** _____disaster_____ . All they wanted to do was attend a reunion with their relatives in Juarez, Mexico. Because they were **(2)** _____transporting_____ a great deal of luggage and many gifts, they decided to rent a van to take them over the border. But the closing of roads for construction forced them to take a **(3)** _____circuitous_____ route to their destination. This made the trip take several hours longer than usual. It wasn't until they were well on their way that they discovered that the air conditioning in the rented van didn't work properly. The air was still and didn't **(4)** _____circulate_____ at all.

This caused a great deal of (5) _____discomfort_____ as they traveled through the hot, dry countryside. But once they arrived at the reunion, their experience was far from (6) _____disagreeable_____ .

C

WRITING SENTENCES Choose two of the words on each line to use in a sentence. You can change the form of the word if you like. (For example, *transport* may be changed to *transportation*, or *circuitous* may be changed to *circuitously*.)

1. **transport   cycle   disaster**

   _____

   _____

2. **circuitous   discontent   amble**

   _____

   _____

3. **transplant   circumference   transition**

   _____

   _____

4. **ambition   disgrace   transform**

   _____

   _____

D

UNDERSTANDING THE WORDS Answer the following questions. Use the boldfaced word in your answer.

1. When would someone need a **transfusion?**

   _____

   _____

2. What do you know about **amphibians?**

   _____

   _____

There are a variety of correct answers. Be sure students' responses reflect an understanding of the meaning of the vocabulary (boldfaced) words.

3. What **disadvantages** do people have without a good education?

_____

_____

4. What sights would you see on a **transcontinental** car trip from California to Florida?

_____

_____

5. What would you say to someone who was **discouraged** because her favorite team lost the championship?

_____

_____

E **TEST-TAKING STRATEGIES** To solve an **analogy,** you need to have the two word pairs related in the same way.

Strategy: Remember that there are different kinds of relationships that an analogy can have. Some of them are synonyms, antonyms, "someone who is" or "something that is," and "type of."

oak : tree :: _____ : building

(A) plant   (B) shed   (C) maple   (D) carpenter

An oak is a type of tree, so read this analogy as, "Oak is a type of tree, and 'blank' is a type of building." Then look for the word that fits in the analogy. (A shed is a type of building.)

Directions: Fill in the bubble next to the word that fits in each analogy.

1. disagreeable : agreeable : : _____ : advantage

(A) friendly   (B) disadvantage   (C) discharge   (D) discourage

2. wolf : vertebrate : : frog : _____

(A) mammal   (B) toad   (C) backbone   (D) amphibian

3. change : transform : : _____ : discontent

(A) content   (B) alter   (C) unhappiness   (D) discomfort

As you review the answers with students, have them explain how they arrived at their answers.

(continued)

4. walk : amble : : _____ : dim

   (A) light bulb (B) fast   (C) around   (D) gloomy

5. disgrace : honor : : _____ : circuitous

   (A) encircle (B) direct   (C) dishonor   (D) round

 TEST-TAKING STRATEGIES On a **multiple-choice** test you are asked to choose an answer by filling in a "bubble."

Strategy: Read the test item with the answer in place to see if you are correct *before* you fill in the bubble.

Directions: Fill in the bubble next to the word or phrase that gives the meaning of the underlined word part.

1. <u>circ</u>ulate   en<u>circ</u>le

   (A) around (B) across   (C) opposite   (D) change

2. <u>trans</u>fusion   <u>trans</u>mitter

   (A) opposite (B) across   (C) around   (D) both

3. <u>dis</u>aster   <u>dis</u>content

   (A) around (B) across   (C) both of   (D) opposite

4. <u>amb</u>le   <u>amph</u>itheater

   (A) across (B) both   (C) opposite   (D) around

5. <u>trans</u>polar   <u>trans</u>port

   (A) opposite (B) across   (C) absence   (D) both

See page 135 for a reproducible test in standardized-test format.

ENRICHMENT WORDS

Draw a line between each Enrichment Word and its definition.

1. transitory   able to use both hands
2. transpose   go around
3. ambidextrous   fall apart
4. circumvent   lasts a short time
5. disintegrate   let out a secret or uncover
6. disclose   reverse position

Word List for Grade 5

abolish	45	discouraged	105	magnificent	25	Spartan (E)	92
academic	89	disgrace	105	maneuver (E)	32	species	49
acute	49	disintegrate (E)	108	marvel	29	spotless	5
ambidextrous (E)	116	dormant (E)	52	medium (E)	36	stealthily	25
ambition	113	drudge (E)	88	mentor	89	stubborn	85
amble	113	dusk	13	Midas touch	89	subculture (E)	68
amphibian	113	elaborate	5	mortal	53	submarine	65
appointed	45	elected	45	myth	53	submerged	65
apprentice	45	emaciated	5	nomad	25	subservient	65
arm	33	encircle	113	nimble (E)	28	subterranean	65
auditory	49	enclose	25	nutritious (E)	52	subzero	65
bicentennial	73	exquisite	5	observant	85	superabundant (E)	68
bilingual (E)	76	fate	53	odious	9	superfluous	65
biped	73	fearless	85	odyssey	89	superheated	65
brawny (E)	8	feast	29	olfactory	49	superimposed	65
candid (E)	12	fool	29	Olympian (E)	56	tactile	49
carriage	45	fragile	5	optimistic (E)	12	tattered	5
chaos (E)	92	frustrated	9	panic	89	timeless	53
charge	33	gloomy	13	plaza	13	transaction	109
circuitous	113	gorge	33	plea	25	transcontinental	109
circulate	113	guarantee	29	predator	49	transform	109
circumference	113	hamlet	13	proclamation (E)	48	transfusion	109
circumvent (E)	116	Herculean	89	prosperous	45	transition	109
colossal	89	homely	5	proverb	93	transitory (E)	112
commonplace	25	honorable	9	prying	85	translate	109
congested (E)	16	illegal	69	psyche	53	transplant	109
convene (E)	48	ill-informed	9	ravine	13	transport	109
counter (E)	36	illogical	69	realm	53	transpose (E)	112
cycle	113	immature	85	rebellion	45	triathlon (E)	76
dash	33	immodest	69	rebuke (E)	32	trilogy	73
deity (E)	56	immortal	53	reckless	85	triple	73
depression	33	immovable	69	representative	45	trivial	73
desperate	9	immune	69	responsive	49	unicellular	73
determined	85	imperfection	69	roam	25	unique	73
dilapidated (E)	16	impersonal (E)	72	roll	33	universe	73
din (E)	28	improper	69	ruefully	25	vegetation	13
disadvantage	105	intolerable	69	scholar (E)	88	vertebrate	49
disagreeable	105	invariably (E)	72	scout	29	vow	29
disaster	105	invincible	53	shiver	29	well-informed	9
discharge	105	lanky	5	shrewd	9	wrench	29
disclose (E)	108	lithe (E)	8	skeptical	89	yarn	33
discomfort	105	looming	13	skirt	33	youthful	85
discontent	105	lush	13	solemn	9		

(E) = Enrichment Words

Test: Lessons 1–5

Directions: Fill in the bubble next to the word that best completes each sentence.

1. The pilot made a(n) _____ attempt to pull the plane out of a dive.
   (A) solemn   (B) odious   (C) desperate   (D) gloomy

2. The clue to the location of the treasure is hidden in the _____ pattern of vines in the painting.
   (A) spotless   (B) elaborate   (C) honorable   (D) emaciated

3. Sarah fell into a deep _____ while she was hiking in the woods.
   (A) ravine   (B) plaza   (C) vegetation   (D) hamlet

4. The _____ taco shells broke in pieces when we tried to eat them.
   (A) tattered   (B) exquisite   (C) fragile   (D) unbreakable

5. Luis would make a good baseball announcer because he's so _____ about the game.
   (A) ill-informed   (B) frustrated   (C) optimistic   (D) well-informed

6. In fairy tales, the _____ servant girl often turns out to be a beautiful princess.
   (A) exquisite   (B) lush   (C) honorable   (D) homely

7. The huge, angry waves _____ up out of the sea frightened Delia as she stood on the beach.
   (A) lapping   (B) looming   (C) homely   (D) desperate

8. A(n) _____ person is someone you can trust.
   (A) honorable   (B) lanky   (C) shrewd   (D) frustrated

9. The campers enjoyed the relaxing calm of the _____ forest.
   (A) spotless   (B) lanky   (C) lush   (D) solemn

10. Many creatures such as bats sleep all day and become active again at _____.
   (A) dusk   (B) dawn   (C) noon   (D) high tide

Enrichment Words

11. The _____ ballerina floated gracefully across the stage.
   (A) brawny   (B) optimistic   (C) dilapidated   (D) lithe

12. The reviewer gave his _____ opinion of the new blockbuster movie.
   (A) dilapidated   (B) candid   (C) congested   (D) desperate

Name

Date

Test: Lessons 1–5, Answers

Directions: Fill in the bubble next to the word that best completes each sentence.

1. The pilot made a(n) _____ attempt to pull the plane out of a dive.
   (A) solemn (B) odious **(C) desperate** (D) gloomy

2. The clue to the location of the treasure is hidden in the _____ pattern of vines in the painting.
   (A) spotless **(B) elaborate** (C) honorable (D) emaciated

3. Sarah fell into a deep _____ while she was hiking in the woods.
   (A) ravine (B) plaza (C) vegetation (D) hamlet

4. The _____ taco shells broke in pieces when we tried to eat them.
   (A) tattered (B) exquisite **(C) fragile** (D) unbreakable

5. Luis would make a good baseball announcer because he's so _____ about the game.
   (A) ill-informed (B) frustrated (C) optimistic **(D) well-informed**

6. In fairy tales, the _____ servant girl often turns out to be a beautiful princess.
   (A) exquisite (B) lush (C) honorable **(D) homely**

7. The huge, angry waves _____ up out of the sea frightened Delia as she stood on the beach.
   (A) lapping **(B) looming** (C) homely (D) desperate

8. A(n) _____ person is someone you can trust.
   (A) honorable (B) lanky (C) shrewd (D) frustrated

9. The campers enjoyed the relaxing calm of the _____ forest.
   (A) spotless (B) lanky **(C) lush** (D) solemn

10. Many creatures such as bats sleep all day and become active again at _____.
    (A) dusk (B) dawn (C) noon (D) high tide

Enrichment Words

11. The _____ ballerina floated gracefully across the stage.
    (A) brawny (B) optimistic (C) dilapidated **(D) lithe**

12. The reviewer gave his _____ opinion of the new blockbuster movie.
    (A) dilapidated **(B) candid** (C) congested (D) desperate

Test: Lessons 6–10

Directions: Fill in the bubble next to the word that best completes each sentence.

1. The _____ stained-glass windows shone in the sunlight.
   Ⓐ commonplace Ⓑ tattered Ⓒ magnificent Ⓓ rueful

2. The _____ in the snow told the trackers that the wounded deer had stopped there to rest.
   Ⓐ depression Ⓑ yarn Ⓒ dash Ⓓ plaza

3. Always use quotation marks to _____ a person's exact words.
   Ⓐ plea Ⓑ guarantee Ⓒ enclose Ⓓ charge

4. The fox _____ approached the henhouse.
   Ⓐ ruefully Ⓑ scout Ⓒ nomad Ⓓ stealthily

5. Every summer wild rabbits _____ on the lettuce in our garden.
   Ⓐ marvel Ⓑ feast Ⓒ wrench Ⓓ roam

6. It's not healthy to _____ on junk food.
   Ⓐ shiver Ⓑ roll Ⓒ gorge Ⓓ arm

7. The cab driver tried to _____ the city traffic by taking a side road.
   Ⓐ skirt Ⓑ fool Ⓒ rebuke Ⓓ roll

8. Jenna's new mountain bike came with a money-back _____.
   Ⓐ plea Ⓑ vow Ⓒ guarantee Ⓓ charge

9. Jamal felt like a _____ when he discovered that the ghostly thumps were coming from the heating system.
   Ⓐ scout Ⓑ marvel Ⓒ nomad Ⓓ fool

10. Every tool chest should include a good _____.
    Ⓐ wrench Ⓑ yarn Ⓒ vow Ⓓ gorge

Enrichment Words

11. The team couldn't hear the quarterback's signals over the _____ of the cheering crowd.
    Ⓐ counter Ⓑ din Ⓒ medium Ⓓ maneuver

12. Just put the dirty dishes on the _____ next to the sink.
    Ⓐ nimble Ⓑ rebuke Ⓒ maneuver Ⓓ counter

Test: Lessons 6–10, Answers

Directions: Fill in the bubble next to the word that best completes each sentence.

1. The _____ stained-glass windows shone in the sunlight.
   (A) commonplace (B) tattered **(C) magnificent** (D) rueful

2. The _____ in the snow told the trackers that the wounded deer had stopped there to rest.
   (A) depression (B) yarn (C) dash (D) plaza

3. Always use quotation marks to _____ a person's exact words.
   (A) plea (B) guarantee **(C) enclose** (D) charge

4. The fox _____ approached the henhouse.
   (A) ruefully (B) scout (C) nomad **(D) stealthily**

5. Every summer wild rabbits _____ on the lettuce in our garden.
   (A) marvel **(B) feast** (C) wrench (D) roam

6. It's not healthy to _____ on junk food.
   (A) shiver (B) roll **(C) gorge** (D) arm

7. The cab driver tried to _____ the city traffic by taking a side road.
   (A) skirt (B) fool (C) rebuke (D) roll

8. Jenna's new mountain bike came with a money-back _____.
   (A) plea (B) vow **(C) guarantee** (D) charge

9. Jamal felt like a _____ when he discovered that the ghostly thumps were coming from the heating system.
   (A) scout (B) marvel (C) nomad **(D) fool**

10. Every tool chest should include a good _____.
    (A) wrench (B) yarn (C) vow (D) gorge

Enrichment Words

11. The team couldn't hear the quarterback's signals over the _____ of the cheering crowd.
    (A) counter **(B) din** (C) medium (D) maneuver

12. Just put the dirty dishes on the _____ next to the sink.
    (A) nimble (B) rebuke (C) maneuver **(D) counter**

Test: Lessons 11–15

Directions: Fill in the bubble next to the word that best completes each sentence.

1. Through hard work, Mrs. Hessey became the most _____ florist in town.
   (A) appointed (B) prosperous (C) responsive (D) mortal

2. Blind visitors to the museum enjoy the _____ exhibit, which allows them to touch the objects that are displayed.
   (A) acute (B) vertebrate (C) carriage (D) tactile

3. In the _____ of the king, people enjoyed peace.
   (A) realm (B) rebellion (C) fate (D) species

4. The preying mantis is a _____ of harmful insects in the garden.
   (A) myth (B) predator (C) psyche (D) myth

5. Tomás won so many races that he began to feel _____ .
   (A) immortal (B) abolish (C) invincible (D) responsive

6. A cat that doesn't react to a sudden noise may have an _____ problem.
   (A) auditory (B) apprentice (C) olfactory (D) elected

7. As a youth, Benjamin Franklin worked as a printer's _____ .
   (A) vertebrate (B) myth (C) predator (D) apprentice

8. Everyone knew that taking part in the _____ was dangerous.
   (A) myth (B) prosperous (C) psyche (D) rebellion

9. Denmark was the first European nation to _____ the capturing and transporting of people for slavery.
   (A) vow (B) abolish (C) proclaim (D) rebel

10. It was the _____ of Narcissus to be turned into a flower.
    (A) rebellion (B) realm (C) predator (D) fate

Enrichment Words

11. The city decided to _____ an emergency meeting to discuss the wildfire threat.
    (A) convene (B) proclamation (C) deity (D) Olympian

12. My mother insists that I eat a _____ breakfast every day.
    (A) deity (B) dormant (C) nutritious (D) proclamation

Test: Lessons 11–15, Answers

Directions: Fill in the bubble next to the word that best completes each sentence.

1. Through hard work, Mrs. Hessey became the most _____ florist in town.
   Ⓐ appointed   **Ⓑ prosperous**   Ⓒ responsive   Ⓓ mortal

2. Blind visitors to the museum enjoy the _____ exhibit, which allows them to touch the objects that are displayed.
   Ⓐ acute   Ⓑ vertebrate   Ⓒ carriage   **Ⓓ tactile**

3. In the _____ of the king, people enjoyed peace.
   Ⓐ realm   Ⓑ rebellion   Ⓒ fate   Ⓓ species

4. The preying mantis is a _____ of harmful insects in the garden.
   Ⓐ myth   **Ⓑ predator**   Ⓒ psyche   Ⓓ myth

5. Tomás won so many races that he began to feel _____ .
   Ⓐ immortal   Ⓑ abolish   **Ⓒ invincible**   Ⓓ responsive

6. A cat that doesn't react to a sudden noise may have an _____ problem.
   Ⓐ auditory   Ⓑ apprentice   Ⓒ olfactory   Ⓓ elected

7. As a youth, Benjamin Franklin worked as a printer's _____ .
   Ⓐ vertebrate   Ⓑ myth   Ⓒ predator   **Ⓓ apprentice**

8. Everyone knew that taking part in the _____ was dangerous.
   Ⓐ myth   Ⓑ prosperous   Ⓒ psyche   **Ⓓ rebellion**

9. Denmark was the first European nation to _____ the capturing and transporting of people for slavery.
   Ⓐ vow   **Ⓑ abolish**   Ⓒ proclaim   Ⓓ rebel

10. It was the _____ of Narcissus to be turned into a flower.
    Ⓐ rebellion   Ⓑ realm   Ⓒ predator   **Ⓓ fate**

Enrichment Words

11. The city decided to _____ an emergency meeting to discuss the wildfire threat.
    Ⓐ convene   Ⓑ proclamation   Ⓒ deity   Ⓓ Olympian

12. My mother insists that I eat a _____ breakfast every day.
    Ⓐ deity   Ⓑ dormant   **Ⓒ nutritious**   Ⓓ proclamation

Test: Lessons 16–20

Directions: Fill in the bubble next to the word that best completes each sentence.

1. You need to dress warmly before going outside in _____ temperatures.
   (A) submarine   (B) superfluous   (C) subzero   (D) superheated

2. In 1976, Americans held celebrations for their country's _____ .
   (A) trilogy   (B) triple   (C) biped   (D) bicentennial

3. In many states, it's _____ to ride a motorcycle without a helmet.
   (A) illegal   (B) immodest   (C) unique   (D) illogical

4. Jamie claims to be _____ to poison ivy.
   (A) improper   (B) immovable   (C) trivial   (D) immune

5. If you forget to advance the film in that old camera, one picture will be _____ over another.
   (A) immovable   (B) superimposed   (C) submerged   (D) trivial

6. Many _____ bomb shelters were dug in backyards in the 1950s.
   (A) subterranean   (B) unicellular   (C) triple   (D) fragile

7. An animal that is a(n) _____ has two feet.
   (A) imperfection   (B) submarine   (C) biped   (D) submarine

8. For people with allergies, the smell of perfume can be _____ .
   (A) superfluous   (B) unique   (C) intolerable   (D) superheated

9. Some game shows ask questions about _____ information.
   (A) subservient   (B) trivial   (C) illogical   (D) bicentennial

10. Astronomers use giant telescopes to study the _____ .
    (A) subterranean   (B) superimposed   (C) trilogy   (D) universe

Enrichment Words

11. The bare walls of the hospital room looked cold and _____.
    (A) impersonal   (B) invariably   (C) superabundant   (D) subculture

12. People who move from one country to another are often _____.
    (A) invariably   (B) immovable   (C) bilingual   (D) triathlon

Test: Lessons 16–20, Answers

Directions: Fill in the bubble next to the word that best completes each sentence.

1. You need to dress warmly before going outside in _____ temperatures.
   (A) submarine   (B) superfluous   **(C) subzero**   (D) superheated

2. In 1976, Americans held celebrations for their country's _____ .
   (A) trilogy   (B) triple   (C) biped   **(D) bicentennial**

3. In many states, it's _____ to ride a motorcycle without a helmet.
   (A) illegal   (B) immodest   (C) unique   (D) illogical

4. Jamie claims to be _____ to poison ivy.
   (A) improper   (B) immovable   (C) trivial   **(D) immune**

5. If you forget to advance the film in that old camera, one picture will be _____ over another.
   (A) immovable   **(B) superimposed**   (C) submerged   (D) trivial

6. Many _____ bomb shelters were dug in backyards in the 1950s.
   (A) subterranean   (B) unicellular   (C) triple   (D) fragile

7. An animal that is a(n) _____ has two feet.
   (A) imperfection   (B) submarine   **(C) biped**   (D) submarine

8. For people with allergies, the smell of perfume can be _____ .
   (A) superfluous   (B) unique   **(C) intolerable**   (D) superheated

9. Some game shows ask questions about _____ information.
   (A) subservient   **(B) trivial**   (C) illogical   (D) bicentennial

10. Astronomers use giant telescopes to study the _____ .
    (A) subterranean   (B) superimposed   (C) trilogy   **(D) universe**

Enrichment Words

11. The bare walls of the hospital room looked cold and _____.
    (A) impersonal   (B) invariably   (C) superabundant   (D) subculture

12. People who move from one country to another are often _____.
    (A) invariably   (B) immovable   **(C) bilingual**   (D) triathlon

Test: Lessons 21–25

Directions: Fill in the bubble next to the word or phrase that best completes each sentence.

1. When the dam broke, a _____ wall of water rolled downstream.
   - (A) fearless
   - (B) colossal
   - (C) reckless
   - (D) Herculean

2. Say, "Look before you leap!" to someone planning to _____.
   - (A) go home
   - (B) eat dinner
   - (C) hike
   - (D) do something risky

3. If you are _____, you might make a good scientist or detective.
   - (A) observant
   - (B) immature
   - (C) prying
   - (D) academic

4. "Birds of a feather flock together" refers to _____.
   - (A) people who hate birds
   - (B) owls
   - (C) people with similar interests
   - (D) people with nothing in common

5. People say that Paul has a _____ because he is always finding money.
   - (A) mentor
   - (B) panic
   - (C) Midas touch
   - (D) proverb

6. "Never leave till tomorrow that which you can do today" is about _____.
   - (A) going to bed early
   - (B) doing things right away
   - (C) taking out the trash
   - (D) growing up

7. Training a puppy requires a gentle but _____ attitude.
   - (A) stubborn
   - (B) skeptical
   - (C) odyssey
   - (D) determined

8. "Don't judge a book by its cover" is advice about _____.
   - (A) looking beyond appearances
   - (B) choosing picture books
   - (C) making quick decisions
   - (D) library research

9. "Great oaks from little acorns grow" refers to the fact that _____.
   - (A) oaks are big trees
   - (B) oaks are bigger than acorns
   - (C) great things often start out small
   - (D) acorns come from big oak trees

10. You might say, "A stitch in time saves nine" to someone who _____.
    - (A) sews too much
    - (B) counts her money
    - (C) saves pennies
    - (D) puts things off

Enrichment Words

11. The town was in _____ after the tornado blew through.
    - (A) drudge
    - (B) Spartan
    - (C) scholar
    - (D) chaos

12. The _____ room looked bare and uncomfortable.
    - (A) scholar
    - (B) Spartan
    - (C) drudge
    - (D) chaos

Test: Lessons 21–25, Answers

Directions: Fill in the bubble next to the word or phrase that best completes each sentence.

1. When the dam broke, a _____ wall of water rolled downstream.
   - (A) fearless
   - (B) colossal
   - (C) reckless
   - (D) Herculean

2. Say, "Look before you leap!" to someone planning to _____.
   - (A) go home
   - (B) eat dinner
   - (C) hike
   - (D) do something risky

3. If you are _____, you might make a good scientist or detective.
   - (A) observant
   - (B) immature
   - (C) prying
   - (D) academic

4. "Birds of a feather flock together" refers to _____.
   - (A) people who hate birds
   - (C) people with similar interests
   - (B) owls
   - (D) people with nothing in common

5. People say that Paul has a _____ because he is always finding money.
   - (A) mentor
   - (B) panic
   - (C) Midas touch
   - (D) proverb

6. "Never leave till tomorrow that which you can do today" is about _____.
   - (A) going to bed early
   - (C) taking out the trash
   - (B) doing things right away
   - (D) growing up

7. Training a puppy requires a gentle but _____ attitude.
   - (A) stubborn
   - (B) skeptical
   - (C) odyssey
   - (D) determined

8. "Don't judge a book by its cover" is advice about _____.
   - (A) looking beyond appearances
   - (C) making quick decisions
   - (B) choosing picture books
   - (D) library research

9. "Great oaks from little acorns grow" refers to the fact that _____.
   - (A) oaks are big trees
   - (C) great things often start out small
   - (B) oaks are bigger than acorns
   - (D) acorns come from big oak trees

10. You might say, "A stitch in time saves nine" to someone who _____.
    - (A) sews too much
    - (C) saves pennies
    - (B) counts her money
    - (D) puts things off

Enrichment Words

11. The town was in _____ after the tornado blew through.
    - (A) drudge
    - (B) Spartan
    - (C) scholar
    - (D) chaos

12. The _____ room looked bare and uncomfortable.
    - (A) scholar
    - (B) Spartan
    - (C) drudge
    - (D) chaos

Test: Lessons 26–30

Directions: Fill in the bubble next to the word that best completes each sentence.

1. Sam was in great _____ after he was hurt in a bicycle accident.
   (A) transplant (B) amphibian (C) discomfort (D) transaction

2. It was Amy's bad luck to have the most _____ person in class as a seatmate for the bus trip.
   (A) discouraged (B) determined (C) transition (D) disagreeable

3. With a can of paint and some new furniture, I could _____ my room.
   (A) amble (B) transaction (C) transplant (D) transform

4. Alicia felt _____ when she finally reached the top of the ridge and saw how much farther she still had to walk.
   (A) circulate (B) cycle (C) discouraged (D) encircle

5. Moving from the city to the country is a big _____.
   (A) transition (C) circumference
   (B) discharge (D) transcontinental

6. Leonard's _____ is to become a successful mystery writer.
   (A) encircle (B) cycle (C) ambition (D) transition

7. Volunteers helped the people in the path of the flood _____ their belongings to higher ground.
   (A) amble (B) transport (C) disaster (D) circulate

8. Should we take the boring, direct road to the farm or the more interesting, _____ road?
   (A) disagreeable (B) circuitous (C) disadvantage (D) amphibian

9. For homework, I had to _____ the story I wrote in English into French.
   (A) transaction (B) transfusion (C) translate (D) cycle

10. The dog team's lack of experience was a major _____ in the long sled race.
    (A) cycle (B) discharge (C) odyssey (D) disadvantage

Enrichment Words

11. Ralph is a troublemaker who is always trying to _____ the rules.
    (A) circumvent (B) disintegrate (C) disclose (D) ambidextrous

12. Blurred vision is just a(n) _____ effect of the eye drops.
    (A) ambitextrous (C) transitory
    (B) transpose (D) circumvent

Test: Lessons 26–30, Answers

Directions: Fill in the bubble next to the word that best completes each sentence.

1. Sam was in great _____ after he was hurt in a bicycle accident.
   - Ⓐ transplant
   - Ⓑ amphibian
   - **Ⓒ discomfort**
   - Ⓓ transaction

2. It was Amy's bad luck to have the most _____ person in class as a seatmate for the bus trip.
   - Ⓐ discouraged
   - Ⓑ determined
   - Ⓒ transition
   - **Ⓓ disagreeable**

3. With a can of paint and some new furniture, I could _____ my room.
   - Ⓐ amble
   - Ⓑ transaction
   - Ⓒ transplant
   - **Ⓓ transform**

4. Alicia felt _____ when she finally reached the top of the ridge and saw how much farther she still had to walk.
   - Ⓐ circulate
   - Ⓑ cycle
   - **Ⓒ discouraged**
   - Ⓓ encircle

5. Moving from the city to the country is a big _____.
   - **Ⓐ transition**
   - Ⓑ discharge
   - Ⓒ circumference
   - Ⓓ transcontinental

6. Leonard's _____ is to become a successful mystery writer.
   - Ⓐ encircle
   - Ⓑ cycle
   - **Ⓒ ambition**
   - Ⓓ transition

7. Volunteers helped the people in the path of the flood _____ their belongings to higher ground.
   - Ⓐ amble
   - **Ⓑ transport**
   - Ⓒ disaster
   - Ⓓ circulate

8. Should we take the boring, direct road to the farm or the more interesting, _____ road?
   - Ⓐ disagreeable
   - **Ⓑ circuitous**
   - Ⓒ disadvantage
   - Ⓓ amphibian

9. For homework, I had to _____ the story I wrote in English into French.
   - Ⓐ transaction
   - Ⓑ transfusion
   - **Ⓒ translate**
   - Ⓓ cycle

10. The dog team's lack of experience was a major _____ in the long sled race.
    - Ⓐ cycle
    - Ⓑ discharge
    - Ⓒ odyssey
    - **Ⓓ disadvantage**

Enrichment Words

11. Ralph is a troublemaker who is always trying to _____ the rules.
    - **Ⓐ circumvent**
    - Ⓑ disintegrate
    - Ⓒ disclose
    - Ⓓ ambidextrous

12. Blurred vision is just a(n) _____ effect of the eye drops.
    - Ⓐ ambitextrous
    - Ⓑ transpose
    - **Ⓒ transitory**
    - Ⓓ circumvent

Class Record Sheet

Class _____ Teacher _____

Tests for Lessons

Student	1–5	6–10	11–15	16–20	21–25	26–30
1						
2						
3						
4						
5						
6						
7						
8						
9						
10						
11						
12						
13						
14						
15						
16						
17						
18						
19						
20						
21						
22						
23						
24						